Customary Laws and Women in Manipur

JWP PUBLICATIONS

Status of Rural Women in India
Status of Nurses in India
Status of Women in the Quran (Urdu)
Status of Single Women in India
Status of Banjara Women
Trafficking of Women and Children in India
Women in Organised Movements
Child Labour in Bangalore City
A Socio-economic Survey of Slum Dwellers in Calcutta
Women's Decade (An Assessment)
The Problem of Dowry in Bangalore City
Indian Women in Media
Women and Law
The Devadasi Problem (English & Kannada)
Changes in the Christian Personal Laws
The Basavi Cult
Christian Marriage and the Customary Practices in Manipur
The Shahbano Controversy
Women in CNI Diocese of Delhi
Wake Up and Live!
A Female Sexuality in Hinduism
Women's Participation in Political Parties in U. P. (Hindi)
Kardwah Such (Hindi)
Women in the Freedom Struggle (Hindi)
The Authority of the Religions and the Status of Women
Pavement Dwellers of Calcutta
Muslim Women
Women and Mass Media
Good News for Women (English, Hindi, Tamil, Telugu, Kannada, Bengali)
Women in Praise and Struggle (English, Hindi, Gujrati, Malayalam)
Vision and Service (English, Hindi)
Legalisation of Prostitution
Shakti Rupa (Hindi Stories and Poems)
Female Children in Fishing Occupation
Status of Indian Women

Status of Women Series

Customary Laws and Women in Manipur

Edited

Jyotsna Chatterji

A Joint Women's Programme Publication

UPPAL PUBLISHING HOUSE

New Delhi 110 002

UPPAL PUBLISHING HOUSE
3 Ansari Road, Daryaganj, Delhi- 110002

For
William Carey Study and Research Centre
14/2 Sudder Street, Calcutta 700 016
and
Joint Women's Programme

ISBN 81- 85565 - 69 -4

Printed in India
Published by UPPAL PUBLISHING HOUSE
3, Ansari Road, Daryaganj, New Delhi 110002
and Printed at ARORA Offset Press,

PREFACE

The book - *Customary Laws and Women in Manipur* - is a collection of valuable articles presented at a seminar organised by Joint Women's Programme on the Customary Laws and Status of Women in Manipur. Customary Laws have been institutionalised by the Village Council or Village Organisation under the leadership of the Chieftain with his Council of Ministers (popularly called the *Haosa System)*. The Village Council is composed of persons of wisdom, integrity and knowledge of Customary Laws. They are nominated by the office of the (*Haosa*) Village Chief. They remain in office as long as the *Haosa* is pleased.

The *Haosa System* has come to stay as an institution. It is the perennial source of customs and tradition, in that, in spite of the onslaught of modernism and advancement in all walks of life, they are able to inherit a rich cultural and traditional heritage. The *Haosa System*, be it on matters relating to economic, political, religious, judiciary, etc., has its bases on the proper interpretation of the customary law and tradition.

The Village Chief functions within the territorial jurisdiction where the village is the highest independent political unit. The *Haosa System* wields political authority and prerogative over the villagers in absolute terms. The Village Chief holds the supreme political power, economic control and supervision of social behaviour and norm. The position of the Village Chief is not elective but hereditory and it passes on from father to the eldest son with only one exception. Among the Lushai Kukis, the office of the Village Chief passes from the father to the youngest son. Such a person can easily turn himself into a despot. But it happens rarely. The primitive state is not tyrannical to its subjects because the first and foremost, we know, that a primitive tribe is always a body of people related by bonds of kinship and relationship; practically, everybody is related to everybody else in the village.

Unlike the Nagas, the Kukis have no right over the land whatsoever. Only with permission from the Village Chief, who is the legal owner of landed properties, the villagers can cultivate the land and utilise other economic resources, including hunting wild life on payments either in cash or kind. Together with such rights of holding immovable properties, the *Haosa System* has certain obligations to the villagers. In return to the services rendered by the villagers free of charges and tributes paid by them as tokens of loyalty, recognition, obedience and solidarity, the *Haosa System* has to protect the interests of the villagers by providing security socially, politically and economically. It is also the bounden duty of the system to see that every villager is protected from external aggression, harm and danger.

The Village Chief is the head of a big family in times of war and peace. The villagers have the right to leave the village and to migrate elsewhere in case the *Haosa System* is found failing in the duty to protect the interests of the villagers.

The Village Council is an autonomous body of representatives from every class. It is in a sense a democratic institution though the members are not elected. The Village Council is an open *darbar*. The Village Chief alone can pronounce the judgement. There had been occasions in the history of Tangkhul tribe when women had become members of the Village Council and represented the spokesperson of the village for a very simple reason that those had better knowledge of language, customary laws and the technique of conversation.

The Convenor or Secretary (*Khawsam* or *Lhangsam Pa*) of the Village Council holds greater responsibility than the designation dictates. He convenes meeting or implements the decision of the Council. The tasks given to him are not specific. He may be asked to act in any capacity such as emissary, negotiator, mediator, depending upon his personal talent.

The *Thiempu* is the office of the village priest or medicine man. In fact, he is the Counsellor-in-charge of public health. This office is very often regarded as hereditory because the secrets of the medicine are not revealed to each and every person. Thiempus generally prefer to teach their sons and grandsons the secrets of the words. The

Thiempu will attend to all the villagers in time of sickness and he officiates on social and religious occasions. The Thiempu is so important in the life of the villagers that for an ordinary observer he seems to be the head of the village, because on every occasion - temporal and religious - he takes precedence over the *Haosa System*.

Thih - kehng Pa (Blacksmith) is the office of the village blacksmith. The office goes to the person who has the highest detexterity in blacksmithy. He is the authorised blacksmith of the village. Everything he does is free of charges. He makes agricultural implements and manufactures weapons. He receives symbolic payment from the villagers at times.

Lawm (Village Labour Corps) - The functions of *Lawm* are concerned mainly with the economic life of the village. All the able-bodied men and women of the village join the organisation irrespective of age and sex. Any household of the village can requisition the services of the *Lawm*. It is an organisation in which young people learn the sense of duty and dignity of labour.

Swam (Bachelors' or Village Youths' Dormitory) - It is a bachelors' dormitory in which all the young boys of the village sleep together at night. Although the main purpose of this organisation is to defend the village community whenever required. It is also an organisation for recreation of the boys. It efficiently mobilises the village youths for defence purposes. They also learn social customs and manners. It serves as an institution of learning, disciplines and other essential characters necessary for a man in future life.

Since the time of the British, the system of *Haosa* and prerogatives have lost favour considerably, with the introduction of the Village Authority Act, 1956, in Manipur, the village organisation under the leadership of the *Haosa* is the ex-officio Chairman of the Village Authorities. The members are no longer nominated by the *Haosa System* but are elected by the villagers themselves through ballot system. Villagers are no longer governed by their customary laws, but are administered by the Village Authority Act, 1956.

Status of Women

The family is under patriarchal control and the first son being the eldest of the family; and women have no right to her father's immovable properties. But any amount of movable properties and wealth she can receive at the pleasure of her parents. A Tangkhul woman (*Yorla*) cannot inherit her father's properties. Yet she is the defender of her father's lineage. But she does inherit properties of her father-in-law through her husband. A poor girl married to a rich man became a rich woman over night.

The eldest son of a family by virtue of his birth, shall represent his clan to the Council. Both men and women are permitted to speak and plead for a relative who is a party in a case. The elders give protection to their younger brothers and sisters in the family matters. Women have no standing with Village Council. Nevertheless, women enjoy respect from elders.

The marriage for a man is with his mother's brother's daughter while for a girl it is with the father's sister's son. But marriage of a girl to her mother's clan is possible for women only after two generations as a rule. The clan system is drawn from father's side. The first son of the father will inherit all the land and property of the family. The daughter has no right to inherit even if she is the first born of the family. All the customary laws, rites and ceremonies are performed in the name of the eldest son only.

In fact, there are no holidays for Kuki women. She has to get up early in the morning and to keep herself busy whole day with domestic chores. The husband does not help her in her domestic work. Kuki women consider weaving and spinning wheel as a special holiday.

The girl has to marry the boy chosen by her parents and her bride price is fixed by his parents. Women are considered as maidservants on sojourn in her husband's family. Men consider women as merely child-bearers. There is no equality between men and women due to bride price. After the death of her husband she is a widow who returns to her parents because she does not consider herself as a true member of her husband's family.

Marriage feast is performed in the house of the bride. When a man and his wife go together, the wife will take the lead and husband goes trailing behind. To walk before a woman is a shameful act on the part of the man. Women are given all protection. A woman married to a man belonging to another village is known as *Pukreila* under customary laws; a *Pukreila* is a free woman. A woman loses her dignity from the day she is married.

Pukreila is a citizen of her father's village as well as of her husband's. Even during a conflict, a *Pukreila* can move freely between the warring villages. The Customary Law states: "you shall not harm a *Pukreila*. In conflict between two villages, a *Pukreila* acts as a mediator. She takes her husband's word to her father and again she brings her father's word to her husband for a peaceful solution of the conflict. In the event when neither of the two camps refused to surrender and when the loss of lives is heavy, then, and there, a *Pukreila* has her prerogative to intervene.

The love marriage is prevalent while elopement is not encouraged. Virgin's Dance is a secret declaration of virginity that is the only thing her husband demands of her. Since the Virgin Dance half-naked in the open field, this is the best time for the young people to select the most beautiful girl of the year at the youth festival. This may be compared to the crowning of beauty queen of the modern world. Among the Tangkhul, woman is the purest of all. No man even dreams of dishonouring his fiance. In short, women are given a very respected place. For a Komren husband, wife is his partner and he does not consider her as inferior. Under the prevailing customary laws, if a husband divorces his wife, he is liable to pay his movable property to his wife. On the other hand, if the wife divorces her husband and if the child is male, he will have the right to inherit father's property.

On the other hand, the Garo Society is basically matrilineal and inheritance is through the female line from mother to daughter. Almost all the tribal societies in the North-East follow the same kind of tradition and often daughters are used to get share of paternal properties along with the sons because while father was setting his house in order before his death felt proper to distribute properties so that no one suffers after him.

The principal concern of Joint Women's Programme has been to study the discriminatory practices and to suggest alternatives in the context of justice in accordance with the provisions of the Indian Constitution. Joint Women's Programme hopes this study will provide inputs in enhancing the cause of gender justice.

December 1, 1995.

JYOTSNA CHATTERJI
Director
Joint Women's Programme

Contents

CHAPTER I

Customary Laws of Tangkhul Tribe

Y.K. Shimray

The Tangkhul is a sub-tribe of the Nagas, inhabiting the entire eastern zone of Manipur, bounded by Burma on the east and Nagaland on the north. The Tangkhul with a population of a little less than 100,000, live on hill tops, ranging from 4,000 to 6,500 feet above the sea. Each Tangkhul village is a composition of 3 or more clans led by their respective leaders, called Wungva (Chieftain). In a village, families of clans live together forming separate colony of their own clan. Thus, a village has 3 or more colonies and is known as Tang.

When they first set out in search of a settlement, the leader (Wungva) of a clan who first raised his fire became the head (chief) of the village. The other leaders remained as Wungvas (chieftains). The chief and the chieftains, together they formed the Village Council which administered all the affairs of their village including political, judicial and defence. Each village is an autonomous state with no appellate court. Only in cases involving two or more villages, the chiefs and chieftains of the villages concerned jointly decide the case. Help may be sought from the Tangkhul Long.

Under the guidance of the Tangkhul Long, each village has their own administrative unit, called Hangnga. Hangnga is the council of the village, and autonomous body, responsible to the village. Customary Laws are constituted on the principles laid down by the Tangkhul Long. Our topic comes under these laws, as follows.

I. Land Ownership

A village has its own village boundaries, marked by natural boundaries, like streams, ranges, low saddles, etc.

The entire area of a village is conveniently divided into three zones. The summit or top portion of the hill is always chosen for settlement. The hillslopes close to the settlement are kept as woodlands, and the low lying area, near the stream is the cultivated area.

As the village has a number of clan — colonies, the wood lands and cultivable lands are also proportionately divided amongst clans, and from the clans amongst the householders. Thus, each and every householder gets his own plots of land for building and cultivation purposes.

The thickly wooded area is reserved and preserved for forestry. For building purposes, any man or woman can freely extract timber from the forest which is called *Khama Ahang* (public land). The land is always in the name of the village Headman.

To preserve the forest, the Village Council enacts an Act, called *Meiyan* (protection from fire). Forest is strictly conserved and preserved under this Act. Any crime, if confessed, can be forgiven or fine reduced to half of the penalty. But no mercy can be shown to the culprit whoever he may be for an offence under this Act of *Meiyan*, intentionally or accidentally. And for the implementation of the said Act, the forest area is divided into number of convenient zones, with each zone under the care of a chieftain (*Wungva*). If fire broke out, and the culprit could not be apprehended, the chieftain in charge of the burnt area shall be held responsible. He has to pay the penalty in place of the culprit.

Roadside trees are planted and carefully conserved. It is believed that people who planted beautiful roadside trees live long. Roadside trees are considered more valuable than the man who fells them. Such a person shall pay the penalty under the Act *Meiyan*. Where garden or jhumming is done, a backfire shall be made along the strategic points.

For the security of the village, sentries are appointed by turns during winter until the first monsoon arrives. This they call *Raikan*. Any defaulter shall be punished under the Act *Meiyan*.

II. Land Use System

Since the village lands are divided and apportioned to each clan at the time of their settlement, the portion of land received by a clan is supposed to be their properties. Hence any portion of land cannot be sold to a person belonging to another clan without the consent of the heir or his family members.

If a person, for an unavoidable reason, is compelled to dispose of his plot of land or cultivation, he shall inform his brothers. Then members of his family shall sit together and fix a minimum rate or price of the land in question. The next kinsman shall be offered. If he cannot afford to buy the land, younger ones shall be given the chance. If none of the brothers is-willing to buy it, then and there, the owner is free to sell it in the open for a higher bargain. However, it is the right of the youngest brother of the family to execute the deal. He is entitled to receive commissions from both parties. This is his birthright, being the youngest of the family.

III. Clan System, Inheritance and Women

Clan means a number of families with a common ancestor under patriarchal control. Hence, the first son is the eldest of the family. The second is second, and so forth. The eldest is the heir to his parents. If he dies without an heir, the second in line shall become the eldest.

Women have no right to her father's properties. There is a saying: *Mayarnao mathameilungna Shanao mazungmuiyana* (Men are rock, women mists). Meaning once a woman gets married, she becomes a member of her husband's family, a different clan (Marriage within the clan is incest). Hence, a woman has no right to inherit her father's landed properties. But any amount of movable properties or wealth she can receive at the pleasure of her parents.

There is one condition under which a woman can enjoy the right to her father's landed properties. That, a man who has no son, with the permission of his heir, can allow his married daughter to use wet rice cultivation so long as she lives. The land shall come back to her father's house at her death.

IV. Village Council/Chieftains

The Village Council is a body of representatives from each and every clan. They are not elected. The eldest of a family, by virtue of his birthright, shall represent his clan to the Council. In the case of big villages, where many members are required to administer the village, sub-chieftains are accepted to represent their respective sub-clans. Chiefship, chieftainship and sub-chieftainship are all hereditary. Since a woman is not an heir to her father's house, her representation in the Village Council is out of the question. However, she has the right to attend the court (*Hangngasheem*) to plead with her family members, especially, in the event of one of her sisters involved in a dispute.

The Village Council is an open *darbar*. Both men and women are permitted to speak and plead for a relative who is a party in a case. They are guided by their representative. After hearing from both parties, as well as from the members of the Council, the Chief or Headman pronounces the judgement. His order is final and binding.

Permanent representation or clan-wise representation to the Council is found most democratic. It has a great impact on the government of the village. In the Council the clan representatives speak for the people, and at home they bring words to their brothers regarding the decisions of the Council. Their colony-wise settlement make it very convenient to spread the news in no time. Thus, all villagers are kept informed of all matters relating to village affairs. Since the elders give protection to their younger brothers, they have full confidence in their leadership in family matters also.

It is true, legally women have no standing in the Village Council. Nor do they have any right to inherit immovable properties from their parents. However, it is a phenomenon that the Tankghul from of old had great respect for women. In speech and in practice, women are given the first place. This can be seen from their daily treatment.

For instance, they say

ava̲ ava	=	mother and father
achon amei	=	ladies and gentlemen
anne awwo	=	mother-in-law and father-in-law
lashiya yarshiyo	=	girls and boys
zarpani	=	sister and brother
siva siva	=	women and men
shanao mayarnao	=	women and men
avva̲ avva	=	female and male
preigahar	=	wife and husband
avva̲ achei	=	mother and brother
ala ava	=	young female, young male
pareinaosan	=	women and children
ava̲kharar avakharar	=	aunt and uncle
ngalashakaza	=	bride-marriage
ngalahangsan	=	bride-engagement
nagalakatha	=	bride procession

ngalasa	=	bride-wedding-feast, etc.
except in the case of		
awo ayi	=	grandpa and grandma

Again, marriage feast is first performed in the house of the bride. They call it *Neirakhamang*. And the final wedding takes place in the groom's house many days after sometimes after nearly one year. During these days the groom stays with his parents-in-law a sort of honeymoon for the new couple.

Whenever a man and his wife go together, the wife will take the lead and her husband goes trailing. This they call *kakachui* (in old days, life was not secure). An attack by wild beast or even by enemy from behind was not uncommon. So the man is all out and risks his life for his wife. He makes his wife feel secure in his presence.

This is true in all circumstances. Whether related or not related, whoever one may be, when a man and a woman or women happen to go together, he will always go after her or them. To walk before a woman is a shameful act on the part of the man. *Kakachui* is a culture. Women are given all possible protection.

V. Customary Laws and Women

The Tangkhul Long constitutes Customary Laws for smooth administration and peaceful coexistence. The Long is a Federation of all the Autonomous Thangkhul Villages.

While making their laws, the Village Council enacts certain provisions to upgrade the dignity of women in their society. These provisions are unique — perhaps, no other is so kind to their womenfolk than Tangkhuls. Some of the provisions are:

i) *Women's Right to Perform Sacrifices*

At the end of the harvest, when all grains are collected and stored in the barn, a special festival is performed. They call in *Chumpha* (opening of barn). It is an inaugural function that marks the beginning of the use of the newly harvested grains.

In the morning on the first day of the festival, the menfolk of the village will jointly clean the water pond, flushing out water, mud, dirts, etc. completely. The pod is kept undisturbed until the next morning. The following morning, at dawn, a woman of high standing will first draw a jar of water from the pond which was cleaned the previous day. If drawn first by an immoral woman, the village is considered under curse through the year, they believe.

That same day the menfolk would collect crabs from the fields or streams and bring them to their wives for the evening sacrifices. The menfolks, after taking their early dinner, will stay out in their farm-sheds. No man above 12 shall remain at home. It is a taboo.

After sunset, when all is dark and calm, the housewife will select the best crabs one male and one female, and wraps them together with a couple of ferns called *Khaireona*. This is again covered with mud. She then performs sacrifices with much prayer to the goddess of wealth, called *Phungjuiphilva*. Late in the night, she buries the crabs in mud into her barn that has been filled with new grains.

At dawn, before the menfolks come back home she will take out some paddy from her barn for use for the first time from the new grains. She will also draw a jar of fresh water from the cleaned pond. She will cook the new grains with this fresh spring-water for the dinner.

The following night too, the menfolks will sleep out in their cultivation sheds. And the womenfolk will cleanse all utensils, crockeries, etc. in the best way they can. Presence of a man in the house during these functions and sacrifices is an abomination, bringing bad or evil fortune to his family throughout the year.

ii) *Pukreila*

A woman married to a man belonging to another village is known as *Pukreil*. Under their Customary Laws, a *Pukreila* is a free woman, a citizen of her father's village as well as of her husband's. Even during a conflict, a Pukreila can move freely between the warring villages. The law says: You shall not harm a *Pukreila*.

As such, when there arises some trouble between the villages of her father and her husband, she can go as mediator. She takes her husband's word to her father and again she brings her father's word to her husband for a peaceful solution.

She can play an important role to bring about peace between the warring camps. There had been many a conflict averted through the goodwill and wisdom of a *Pukreila*. On the other hand, a foolish *Pukreila* can make the situation fall from the frying pan into the fire. Thus, the old saying holds good.

> *"Shanao eina Philawunganao auki tai*
> *Shanao eina sapher khamhor, zamshei*
> *khamaying ngathay"*.

(meaning)

Because of a woman, the chieftains lost their head,

Because of a woman, the best wine and the best food

exchanged in turns.

iii) *Pukreila's Prerogative*

When two villages failed to settle a case, a time is fixed and a place appointed to decide the case by action. All the neighbouring villages shall be informed to witness. On the appointed day, the two camps shall stand in line facing each other within a limited boundary. They stand face to fact and fight with tact and skill The neighbouring villagers, led by Tangkhul Long Leaders, remain watching around the arena. In such a fight, called *Ngasungrai,* they use long javelins. Throwing a javelin against enemy is not permitted. Such an act will amount to losing the case. Any breach of law will not be ignored by the Long.

The defeated party loses the case. If one party retreated, the other party shall not pursue and kill enemy from behind. Again the Tangkhul Long is there to enforce justice. Of course, the retreating party loses the case.

In the event, when neither of the two camps refused to surrender, and when the loss of lives is heavy, then and there, a Pukreila has her prerogative to intervene. Holding her *zeithing* (a traditional iron staff), she goes between the two lines of battle, shouting, *Shaphaira*! *Shaphaira*! (enough, enough)... At her shout, the fight ceases. There shall be no more fighting after this. And that is the end of the fight. And case is compromised.

In the matter of land dispute, the disputed area shall equally be divided between the two parties by the *Longwo* (long chief). Order of the *Longwo* is final and binding. However, the verdict of the *Longwo* comes through the intervention of a Pukreila which is her prerogative.

iv) *Yorla and Varei*

A woman loses her identity from the day she is married. Yet her privilege of being a daughter of her parents remains in the life of the family. In order to reckon this unbreakable ties of a family, they adopt a special link called *Yorla-Varei*

A woman when married becomes a *Yorla* (brother's lineage) and her brother remains as *Varei* (sister's lineage). This lineage is remembered in every important function, like marriage. New building construction, obituary, etc. when there is an important function in the house of her brother, she (*Yorla*) shall bring her privileged share, ranging from ornament to cloth to buffalo. For an obituary, she shall bring a cloth. All *Yorlas* have their due or privileged contributions according to their culture. Likewise, the brother (*Varei*) shall contribute his due share for such important functions and celebrations in the house of his sister (*Yorla*).

The method of reckoning the relationship between the brother and sister goes on from generation to generation. Hence the identity of a clan remains distinct and clear. It becomes a way of life and deeply-rooted culture of the people. A Tangkhul woman *(Yorla)* cannot inherit her father's properties yet she is the defender of her father's lineage.

v) *Changes of Life*

It may sound incredible that a woman is fortunate in that she does not inherit her parents properties. But she does inherit the properties of her father-in-law through her husband. A poor girl married to a rich young man becomes a rich woman overnight. This is what the people call *Mirin Khangatak* (changes of life).

Since Tangkhul brides do not pay dowry, and that love marriage is prevalent, it is not impossible for a woman to become rich by inheriting properties through her husband.

vi) *Best Inheritance of a Woman*

Tangkhuls celebrate their biggest festival, called Luira, in February, marking the beginning of *Sowin*. One of the most outstanding features of *Luira is Lakhanganui* (virgins' dance). The dance is open to only virgins. Hence the name. Customarily, all the virgins in the village shall join the dance. They dance in traditional costume — a skirt, a pair of brass bangles, armlets on both arms, a set of

Kongsang(carnelian beads) to cover her breasts and another set of *Kongsang* over her head.

The dancers move in a circular motion. They sing as they dance, striking their bangles to the beat of the music while the rest of the villagers stand around and watch.

If a virgin refused to join the dance, her character is suspected. She is considered no longer a virgin, and a fine is imposed according to their custom. On the other hand, if one who had lost her virginity, joins the dance for fear of punishment or to hide away her immorality, it is believed that some insect or creature crosses past her while dancing. Such an unfaithful girl cannot go unpunished. If she denied, physical test shall be performed by the members of the Village Council. If proved unfaithful, she shall pay double the fine. Virgins' Dance is a secret declaration of virginity.

Since the Virgins dance half-naked in the open field, this is the best time for the young people to select the Most Beautiful Girl of the year. In big villages where there are a number of virgins, separate dances are organised age-wise or colony-wise to their convenience. Each selected beauty is honoured by making her the Hostess during the festival, called *Yarra* (youth festival) that comes off within a couple of months. It is a big honour, may be compared to the Crowning of a Beauty Queen of the modern world.

Believe it or not, Beauty Contest among the Tangkhuls had been in practice from time immemorial. Yet, *Lakhanganui* (virgin's dance) is much more than a Beauty Contest — it is a secret declaration of virginity also.

Lakhanganui is the highest code of conduct. It makes no virgin ever imagine immorality, nor the man ever dream of dishonouring his fiancee. Among the Tangkhul, woman is the purest of all. Virginity is her immemorial inheritance, and that is the only thing her husband demands of her.

CHAPTER II

Customary Laws of Thadou Kuki Tribe

D.P. Haokip

The study on the Thadou Kuki relates to the time when Assam was in its original shape. During those days, the area of the hilly country bounded by the Angami Naga of Naga Hill District in the north, the province of Burma in the east, the Chin Hills and Lushai Hills in the south and District of Cachar in the west. Their substantial concentration was in the hills of the State of Manipur on all sides of the Imphal valley. The Kukis are generally known as mongoloid tribe.

Willam Shaw of Assam Civil Service has written about these people as he is well equipped to write about them. As the Sub-Divisional Officer of North West area of Manipur state he had lived among the Nagas and the Thadou Kukis for seven years. The book has been very systematically divided into chapters on their customs, habits, manufacture of arms and food habits, law and justice.

Hence short notes on the customary laws of the Thadou Kukis in India are extracted from the book here.

1) **Land ownership** : The (Haosapa) Chief of the Vilage is the authority in the village. All landownership is vested in the hands of the Chief or Haosapa. The powers and functions of the Chief as a landownership are as under:

a) *Changseo* : This is one dan or measure of paddy to the Chief of the Village. Each household pays this to its Chief or Hausa for the right of cultivation annually. Among the Haokips only a jar or *Ju(Vin)* is paid. It is called *Delpeng*.

b) *Khotha : Khotha* is the name given to the free labour applied by one person from each household in the village, who must work one day for the Hausapa of the village in the field annually.

c) *Shel Kotkai* : This is an amount of rupee 1.00 per head paid by the seller of *mithun,* buffalo or cattle to the Haosapa of his village. It is by way of quittance to the Chief for the past grazing on his lands.

d) *Migration of Kichou* : When a household migrates from his village to another village without the permission of the Chief, the Chief has a right to confiscate his property.

e) *Samel* : When a hunter killed an animal by whatsoever means, the right hind leg of the animal goes to the Chief of the village. This means that the Chief is the owner of the land.

f) *Land use system* : Jhumming cultivation is the main profession of the Kukis. The Jungle is cut in January or February annually. It is then allowed to dry thoroughly and is burnt. After that the field is cleared, the sowing begins. So, the harvest season starts in October and ends in early December. Jhumming, which is the name given in Assam to the dry cultivation, is also known as shifting cultivation, because it is shifted every year.

Besides, the land is used by the villagers for hunting, in the forest, and cutting the trees for housing materials, and furniture etc. The Kukis are keen in rearing *mithuns*. So the *mithuns* are set free on the land and they spoil the whole land. This kind of land use system is not desirable.

2) **Clan system** : The Thadou Kukis are patrilineal and exgamous, and their terms of relationship are of course classificatory. The marriage for a man is with his mother's brother's daughter while for a girl it is with her father's sister's son *(Heni)*. But marriage of a girl to her

mother's clan is possible for women only after two generations as a rule.

So, there are two kinds of *Hepu* (grandfather). One is mother's father and the other is father's father *(Hopu)*. This clan system is taken from father's side.

Hepu	-	Grandfather
		Mother's father
		Mother's brother
		Mother's brother's son.
Hepi	-	Grandmother
		Mother's Mother
		Mother's brother's wife
Hepu	-	Grandfather
		Father's father
Hepi	-	Grandmother
		Father's Mother
Heni	-	Father's Sisters
Hegang	-	Father's Sister's husband.

3) Inheritance : As I have quoted above, the first son of the father will inherit all the land and property of the family. The daughter has no right to inherit even if she is the first born of the family. That means women are not allowed to inherit the father's property and land etc.All the inheritance goes by the male-line only and no female has any right to claim as heir of a person.

Firstly, the first born son or daughter shall be named after his or her grand father's or grandmother's (*Hepu* or *Hepi*) name. But in female line there is no hard and fast rule to follow this custom.

Secondly, Sating is the flesh between the upper side of the ribs and the side of all animals killed. It is paid by the brothers to their eldest male — next of kin. Therefore, all the Satings of Paokai and Paosat goes to Goupu, the eldest son of Kailkholam and not only Sating but also all the land owned and property of the father shall be inherited by *Goupu*.

Thirdly, all the customary laws and rites and ceremonies are performed in the house of the eldest son (*Goupu*). Women do not apprear in the lineage of the inheritance law.

4. Village Council chieftainship: Usually, the Kukis select the dense jungle, the top of the ridge or the slope just below for the village site. The Chief or Rausapa is the highest authority in the village. He is the right person to take in and out a house-holder in his village.

Mantri : He is the second highest powerful authority in the village. He is next to the Chief of the Village. On the other hand, the Chief of *Hausapa* is the nominal head of the village, but all the powers are vested in the hands of the *Mantri*.

Priest (Khothempu) : In religious side, *Thempupa* is the highest in the village. All beliefs ceremonies are performed by the priest.

Semang Pachong : is known as Chief's subject. Sometimes, the Chief selected them from each clan in the village. They resemble the village Council members. All the important cases in the village are decided by this *Semang Pachong*. This *Semang Pachong* is the highest authority in the village.

Kholhangsampa: Communicator is the most important person in the Village. At the time of cutting Jhumming field, all the villagers submit their *daos* and weapons and the blacksmith will sharpen all those weapons. In doing so, every householder offers one day's free labour to the field of the blacksmith. This is called as *Thihtha*. Same was the case with the priest. This is also known as *thempu tha*.

Sottol Runner : is like a Chowkidar. He is also called *Khotucha*. The *Semang Pachong* may use him to go here and there as a runner. There is no hard and fast rule to offer one day free labour to him or not. It is on the mercy of the Chief. Women are not included in the village Council.

Status of Women

For Thadou Kuki woman there are no holidays. She has to get up early in the morning to bring water and cook morning meal. At the same time she has to pound paddy to dehusk rice. The husband does not help in her domestic work.

When morning meals are over, she has to prepare packed-lunch for the day time and follow the husband to the jhum. After finishing the day's work for the day she has to carry back firewood and fodder to feed the domestic animals at home. As soon as she reaches home she has to prepare evening meals. After finishing the evening meals, the husband takes rest and sleep soundly. But the women have to dry up wet clothes of the men over charcoal fire at late night. After doing all these, she has to sit at her spinning wheel till late night for the woman is responsible for providing the garments to all her family members. So, it seems that the Thadou Kuki women considers only weaving and spinning wheel as a special holiday.

Regarding marriage, the girl has to marry the boy chosen by her parents and her bride price is fixed by her parents.

Why they do so? Because:-

a) Women are considered as maidservant and on sojourn in her husband's family.
b) Women had a bride-price.
c) Men consider women as merely child-bearers.
d) Husbands consider their wives as slaves.

e) Women are weaker than men.

f) Women think always that they had original home and one day they can go back at the time of their husbands death.

For all these reasons, women are dominated by men and excluded from the inheritance of her husband's properties. I think this is due to of bride-price. The term price makes low status to all women. So long as the phrase bride-price is used, the husbands will consider them like a property which can be moveable or changeable at any time and any moment. Hence it is better to change the term bride-price into marriage bond or gift. In doing so, there shall be equality between men and women in the tribal community.

After the death of her husband, she is a widow who considers herself that she has no more rights in the family and returns to her parents. Moreover, the Thadou Kuki women consider themselves as a slave or a servant. The servant has no right in the family. The servant has no authority even upon his children. The Thadou Kuki women should try to overcome all this thinking and consider themselves as true family members even when their husbands have died or left the house.

Being Christians let us see the Bible. The Old Testament gives many examples of obedient wives and daughters.

The daughter of Zelophehad stood before Moses and requested that they be given their father's inheritance since he had died without a son (Num 27:1-11). Moses granted their petition. As a result of the boldness of these women, the law was altered to allow a daughter to inherit property, if the husband died without son.

If Christianity brings freedom to all mankind it does too to all women as well. To all mankind denotes including women. There is no difference between men and women. All are equal in the eyes of God. So also to man. The women of the Thadou Kukis is now legally entitled to hold property like men and may allow to inherit her husband's property. It depends upon the husband, because the husband is the head of the family.

Lastly, I myself have no son and only one daughter and allowed my daughter to inherit all my properties. No man can forbid it because this is the right of property and the right of the individual enshrined in the Indian constitution.

CHAPTER III

Cheiftainship Among the Kukis

Dr. T.S. Gangte

The traditional political life of the Kukis as a separate institution cannot be studied in isolation. The institution is closely intertwined with other institutions, such as social, religious, economic, etc. A superficial knowledge of the Kuki society will reveal that the institutions of political, social, economic and religious are overlapping one another, and one may draw the conclusion that there is no political institution at all among the Kukis.

Political system or institution among the Kukis, like among other primitive societies, is based on Kinship relations (Schapera, 1963 :1).[1] Mains (London, 1972 :76)[2] observed that:

> All ancient societies regarded themselves as having proceeded from one original stock, and even laboured under an incapacity for comprehending any reason, except this, for

> their holding together in political Union. The history of political idea begins, in fact, with the assumption that kinship in blood is the sole possible ground of community in political functions, nor is there any of those subconscious or feeling, which we term emphatically revolutions, so startling and so complete as the change which is accomplished when some other principle — such as that, for instance, local contiguity — established itself for the first time as the basis of common political action. The idea that a number of persons should exercise political rights in common simply because they happen to live within the same topographical limits was utterly strange and monstrous to primitive antiquity.

Such a system of political institution based on kinship relation is termed as a mere "Social Organisation", which is distinguished from "Political Organisation" of the civilized communities (Morgan, L.H. : 1877 : 6766).[3] Similar views were also expressed by Durkheim, Hobbouse, Vinogradoff, etc. MacIver (New York, 1965 : 119)[4] however said:

> In the primary sense a tribe is community organised on the basis of kinship... and usually claiming to be descended from a common ancestor. Tribal Government is

> characteristic of simple society and is then equivalent to primitive Government.

Yet another anthropologist (Malinowski, B, 1947 :263-66)[5] whose authority on the primitive people was undisputed, said:

> The primitive state is not tyrranical to its subjects because, first and formost, we know that a primitive tribe is always a body of people related by bonds of kinship and relationship, by clanship and age-grade; and he also speaks of the tribe as a group where practically everybody is related, really or factitiously, to everybody else.

The one focal point that has to be highlighted is Chieftainship and the concept of territory among the Kukis. The village is the highest political unit among the Kukis, and Chief of the village and his Council of Ministers which function within a territorial jurisdiction (Gangte, 1982 : 55)[6] wielding its political authority and prerogative over the villagers in absolute terms are the supreme political powers. Schapera (1963 : 14-15) said:

> Each tribe claims exclusive rights to the land it occupies. All people living there are subjects to the Chief, as head of the local Government, and only by moving away can they escape his control. Outsiders may not settle in its territory without his permission; and he places them where he wishes, henceforth they are his subjects, and if they

disobey him they may be expelled. He also regulates the distribution and use of the land.

Chieftainship among the Kukis is associated with the *Upa* or senior man. The term *upa* is conferred on a person by way of reverence, and a great deal of veneration is attached to it. *Upas* are the only persons who can become Chiefs. Thus, Chiefs are synonymous with *upas*.

The term *Naopa* stands for the junior man. *Naopa* cannot in the normal course of the customary law become the Chief. He can become so only with the full consent of the Chief, who is his *Upa*, as also with the concurrence of the Council of Ministers of the Chief, which is known as *Semang Upa* or *Pachong* collectively. Before a *Naopa* can become the Chief, certain formalities and obligations are to be gone through. Under the circumstances, there is limited room for growth of political leadership among the *upas* alone. Unless specifically desired by the *upa to* develop and groom his *Naopa* (literally younger brother) for leadership, there is no chance for the *Naopa* to become the leader or Chief.

Leadership manifests, therefore, in the rights and privileges handed down to the *Upas*, and these prerogatives are institutionalised in Village Organisation and the customary law, through the system of Chieftainship called *Haosa* and its Council of Ministers called *Semang Upa* or

Pachong. Thus, the Chieftainship has come to stay as an institution which is the perennial source of customary laws, and the mechanism by which such laws are interpreted in the social system that makes them a living force enabling to maintain their separate identity inheriting a rich cultural heritage.

A village is an independent political unit among the Kukis, and the Chief of the village and his Council of Ministers are the political leaders. Administration of justice, enforcement of executive functions, maintenance of social practices and customary law, including religious performances are the areas of the village administration under the Chieftainship and his Council of Ministers. Thus, a Kuki village is an important administrative unit.

A Kuki village has inevitably got a Chief, which post is not elective but hereditary. The Chief is assisted in his administration by a team of persons, collectively called *Semang-Upa* or *Pachong* which is similar to the Council of Ministers in modern times. The office of the Chief is hereditary, and is passed on from father to his eldest son, who otherwise is known as "Upa". The office of Chieftainship is called *Haosa* which is vested with so much of power and authority over his subjects that a person in that capacity is often prone to abuse his power and thus turn himself into a despot.

The structure of the village political organisation is as follows:

Administrative Structure of Kuki Chieftainship

HAOSA
(Chieftain)

LHANGSAM	THIH-KHENG	THIEMPU
(Speaker or Secretary)	(Blacksmith)	(Priest)

SAWM	LAWM
(Bachelor's Dormitory)	(Village Labour Corps)

LAWMPI LAWM-LAI LAWM-MEO LAWM-CHANGPAH

Haosa Chief

Haosa is the office of the Village Chief. It is hereditary, passing from father to the son. The Office is occupied only by the *Upas* except among the Lushai Kukis which goes from father to youngest son. Among the Kukis, and unlike the Nagas, *Haosa* has the absolute right of ownership of the entire land of the village. The villagers have no right over the land whatsoever. Even if a villager, who is generally a *Naopa* wishes to establish a new village, he can do so only with the permission of the *Haosa*. However, absolute his right over the land might be, normally allows, in consultation with his Council of Ministers, the villagers to cultivate and utilise as per their requirements. But the villagers have to pay to the *Haosa* in return for such privileges in the shape of tributes called

Changseo, even of the part of hunted games called *Saleng*. *Changseo*, is payable annually after harvest. The *Haosa* is also entitled to free labour of each villager once in a year called *Khou-Tha*.

Together with such rights, the *Haosa* has certain obligations to the villagers. In return to the services rendered by the villagers free of cost and the tributes paid as tokens of loyalty, recognition, obedience and solidarity, the *Haosa* has to protect their interests by providing security socially, politically and economically. It is also the bounden duty of the *Haosa* to see that every villager is protected from external aggression and danger.

The *Haosa* system is very similar to the Social Contract Theory of Hobbes who enunciated that rights imply duties. By this system both the villagers on the one hand and the *Haosa* on the other are duty-bound to fulfil their rights and obligations towards each other.

The *Haosa* wields a great deal of authority over the villagers who are mostly his kin group and junior to him by descent. He is assisted in his day-to-day administration by a Council. In short, he is the head of a big family in times of war and peace. Although he is the legal owner of the land, the *Haosa* owns little and he administers the village according to the advice given by the elders of the Council. Many writers having a superficial knowledge about the men and affairs try to draw a similarity between the *Haosas and the Zemindars* and often jump to a conclusion that the system of *Haosa* is despotic. Of course, there is sufficient room for a *Haosa* to become despotic and tyrannical, but it happens very rarely. Despite such possibility of being so dreaded by the villagers, there are thousand and one ways by which such a situation can be averted due to interaction of forces within the system. The villagers are at liberty to leave the village and migrate elsewhere in case the *Haosa* is found failing in his duty to protect the interest of the villagers. This happens to be the main factor that contributes to the nomadism of the Kukis.

The *Haosa* system is indeed very firmly entrenched among the Kukis. Notwithstanding the inherent defects associated with the *Haosa* system which the Kukis cannot do away with, there are some merits also in this system to set-off the evils in it. The *Haosa* system has come to stay as a perennial source of custom and tradition, in that, in spite of the onslaught of modernism and advancement in all walks of life, they are able to inherit a rich cultural and traditional heritage. The *Haosa system,* be it on matters relating to economical, political, religious, judiciary, etc. has its bases on the proper interpretation of the customary law and tradition.

Unlike the Nagas of Manipur who have no permanent and strongly established secular head of a village, the office of which is usually held by an elected man called "Gaonbura" for a specified term, and also the Nuer tribes of Africa, who do not have a permanent Chief of the village other than the Leopard-skin clad Chief (Evans-Pritchard, 1940 : 163), who, though wields a great deal of influence and acts as a go-between to settle disputes, the Kukis have a very solid established institution of Chieftainship who, being the *Upa* of a particular clan or lineage or sub-lineage, is considered to be the fountainhead of all customs and retainer of tradition. Like the African Nuer (Evan Pritchard, 1940 : 6) the Kuki political structure "..... is segmented into lineages which are diverging branches of descent from a common ancestor"

Thus, the nomenclature of every clan, lineage or sub-lineage, bears the name of each founding father and thereby the members claiming blood relationship of a common ancestor.

On this very kinship genealogy is built the political structure of the Kukis which has been institutionalised in *Haosa*. This is the main reason why the system of *Haosa* could not be given a go-by, despite varied changes all around. The political structure of the Kukis is, therefore, based on kinship hierarchical order of the clan. The Kuki political system has a peculiar way of effective functioning to meet external aggression by expressing kinship solidarity and loyalty despite their inter-clan rivalry and feud.

The institution of *Haosa* does not, and cannot function in isolation. In other words, the institution of *Haosa* presupposes the existence of *Semang Pachong* Council. It has to work through the Council which assists him in his day-to-day administration. This Council is composed of persons of wisdom, integrity, knowledge of customary law etc. and are nominated by the *Haosa*. Special representation is always given from the minorities and the poor villagers in the Council. The Council members assemble and make deliberations. They remain in office as long as the *Haosa* is pleased. Social, political, economical, judicial matters etc. are dealt with by the Council.

The main mechanism through which the Council exercises its administration is the interpretation of the customary laws. The *Haosa* as the Chairman or head of this Council and presides over the meetings. The members of the Council are exempted from payment of all kinds of tributes levied on the common villagers in recognition of their services.

The components of the Council are as follows:

Khawsam or Lhangasam Pa

He is the spokesman (Convenor or Secretary) of the Council. Literally speaking, he is the councillor in charge of information and broadcasting. In reality, he holds greater responsibility than the designation indicates. He convenes meeting of the Council, conveys decisions of the Council to the general public and enforces or implements the decisions of the Council. The tasks given .to him not specific. He may be asked to act in any capacity, such as emissary, negotiator, mediator depending upon his personal talent.

Thiempu

Thiempu is the office of the village priest or medicine man. Literally speaking, he is the councillor in charge of public health in the true sense of the term. Persons for this office are chosen from among those who know the *Thiem-Thu* (the secret words of medicine). This office is very often regarded as hereditary because the secrets of the medicines are not revealed to each and every person. Thiempus generally prefer to teach their sons and grandsons the secrets of the words. Moreover, to learn this secret costs a lot of money and time. Therefore, very few persons bother to master this knowledge.

The *Thiempu* will attend to all the villagers in times of sickness, and he officiates on social and religious occasions. The *Thiempu* is so important in the life of the Kukis that for an ordinary observer he seems to be the head of the village, because on every occasion — temporal and religious — he takes precedence over the *Haosa*. For example, wine (*zu*) is very important in the life of the Kukis. Therefore, on every occasion wine is served in order or social position and seniority in age. Irrespective of the fact that he is junior or lower in status, the *Thiempu* will be served the wine first on social and religious occasions. The office of the *Thiempu*, more or less, enjoys autonomy from that of *Haosa* and his Council. He treats all the ailing villagers, free of cost. In return, he is allowed to collect his *Changseo* i.e., bucket of paddy paid as a tribute to the *Haosa* and the *Thiempu*, annually. This is paid in acknowledgement of his services for the welfare of the village community. But the rate of *Changseo* he receives annually is lower than that of the Chief. *Thiempu* is also entitled to a share of the wild game hunted and brought by the villagers. This share is called *Thicm-Sha* (Meat-share of the secret word). This share is not the same as the *Haosa* receives by way of *Samal* or *Saleng*. It is connected with the religious belief.

Thih-Kehng Pa (Blacksmith)

Thih-Kheng is the office of the village blacksmith. This office goes to the person who has the highest dexterity in blacksmithy. He is the authorised blacksmith of the village. He does not charge for what he makes for individual villagers. Everything is done free of cost. He makes agricultural implements, such as hoes, axes, spades etc.. and manufactures weapons like swords, arrows, guns, bullets, etc. In recognition of his services, he is given *Changseo* by all the villagers annually, but the rate will be lower that is received by the *Haosa*. Just as the *Thiem-Sha* is given to the

Thiempu, *Thih-Kheng* is also given *Thih-Kheng-sha* (Meat share of the blacksmith) by every hunter. This is a symbolic payment to the *Thih-Kheng* for having manufactured the bullet for the hunters.

Lawm (Village Labour Corps)

The functions of *Lawm* are concerned mainly with the economic life of the village. All the able-bodied men and women of the village join his organisation, irrespective of age and sex. Any household of the village can requisition the services of the Lawm. All the villagers, therefore, are to join the Lawm. The number will be credited to his name and the same number of work he thus earns will be repaid to him by other members with labour. In this way, the *Lawm* members reciprocate in helping each other and keeping the village, as far as possible, self-sufficient in the matter of physical labour.

Sometimes their *Lawm* can be hired by any villagers or Chief. In return, they are given food and drink. But this entertainment needs not be instantaneous. It may be on a later day when the person who engages the *Lawm* is in a position to repay. It is an organisation in which training for leadership is given to the young people of the village. It is also an organisation in which the young ones learn a sense of duty and dignity of labour. This organisationn is in a way connected with the *Thih-kheng* office, because the success or failure of the organisation depends upon the ability of the *Thih-Kheng* to produce and to provide implements.

Changes

Since the time of the British, the feudal system of *Haosa* and its prerogatives have lost their favour considerably. Consequent upon the developmental schemes taken up during the post-independence days in the country, the institution of *Haosa* has shown further changes. Its importance has greatly declined, and the effectiveness of the institution and its authority waned.

With the introduction of the Village Authority Act, 1956 in Manipur, the village organisation under the leadership of the *Haosa* is the ex-officio Chairman of the Village Authorities. The members are no longer nominated by the *Haosa*, but are elected by the villagers themselves, through ballot system. This system has given birth to different parties within a village and, therefore, the village as a single unit could not be cohesive. The solidarity of the whole village which used to be the backbone of the political system is utterly shattered.

Villagers are no longer governed by their customary laws, but are administered by the Village Authority Act. The Act says that the villagers have direct participation in the village government and the villagers are the persons who run the machinery of the Government. This new system indeed sounds very well and the people are enthusiastic about giving a fair trial to it.

Moreover, with the infiltration of a number of Christians, the Kukis are now more inclined to make a departure from their traditional social norms of life. This trend has further been accelerated by the spread of education, and mobility of the rural population to the urban areas for enjoying greater amenities of life available there.

The Village Chief cannot officially or openly enjoy age-old prerogatives, such as tributes of *Saleng* (Samal), *Salu, Changseo, Khuotha,* etc. now. Unless the village authorities decide that the *Haosa* has to be given the annual traditional tributes, the *Haosa* has to manage without such privileges. As for *Khuomuol* and its importance, it still holds good. While *Khuojeh, Unmit* etc., rites to ward off epidemics and other village cleansing ceremonies are no longer in vogue, as Christianity has supplanted them all, the same are still practised in non-Christian villages.

Swam (Bachelors' or Village Youths Dormitory)

Swam among the Kukis is the name of the other youth organisation which concerns only able-bodied young boys of the village. It is a bachelors' dormitory in which all the young boys of the village sleep together at night. The nature of hostility and practice of tribal raids necessitate the existence of this organisation, so that in times of emergency the services of all the able-bodied men might be available at short notice. They have to offer their free and compulsory services to the village. Although the main purpose of this organisation is to defend the village from external dangers, in times of peace they render every possible service to the village community whenever required. Moreover, it is an organisation for recreation of the young boys. In the *Swam*, younger boys are taught all sorts of things, from cutting jokes to taking responsibilities. Stories are told by the elder members and sometimes topics ranging from girls to war become the subject matters of great interest. This organisation is also connected with the *Thin-Kheng* office, because the efficient mobilisation of the village youths for defence depends mainly upon his ability of the *Thin-Kheng* to produce weapons.

This organisation may be likened with that of Defence and Home Department of Modern Administration.

The Kuki society is such that during the days when inter-tribal feuds were a part of their way of life, every able-bodied youth of a village slept together so that they might be readily available for deployment in times of emergency. This place is also considered place of learning. Boys of different age-groups who are assigned various jobs and other sundry chores stay together. The boys of younger age-groups learn the things from the older groups. They also learn social customs and manners. It serves as an institution of learning, discipline and other essential characters necessary for a man in future life. It has thus been considered as a very essential part of the village administration among the Kukis. This is an organisation responsible for mobilisation of the services of the young men to meet the exigencies of the society. In this connection Roy (1918:218)[10] describes the bachelors' organisation as:

> ....archaic form of economic, social and religious organisation. It must have been an effective economic organisation for purposes of food quest, a useful seminary for training young men in their social and other duties, and an institution for magico-religious observances calculated to secure success in hunting and to augment the preventive power of the young men so as to increase the number of hunters in the tribe.

Thus, the young boys of the village are concentrated at a place for emergency service.

REFERENCES

1. Schapera I, 1963 Government and Politics in Tribal Societies, London.
2. Mains, H.S. 1972 The Ancient Law, London.
3. Morgan, L.H. 1877 The Ancient Society, London.
4. MacIver, R.R. 1965 The Web of Government, New York
5. Malinowski, B. 1947 Freedom and Civilisation, London
6. Gangte, L.S. 1982 Zomi Polity in Transition, J.N.U., New Delhi.
7. Schapera, I 1963 Government and Politics in Tribal Society, London.
8. Evans Pritchard, E.E.1940 The Nuer, London.
9. Ibid.
10. Roy S.C. 1918 The Oraon, Ranchi.

CHAPTER IV

Komrem Tribe

S. Serto

The Komrem tribe consists of five sub-tribes which are recognised tribes in Manipur. The sub-tribes are Kom, Aimol, Chiru, Koireng and Purum. The Komrem tribes are scattered all over Manipur but mainly concentrated in Churachandpur, Senapati, Tamenglong and Chandel districts.

Language : The sub-tribes which consist the Komrem tribe speak basically one language but slightly different dialects. Being dynamic the language continued to develop over the years and this is the reason why the Komrem sub-tribes have developed their own dialects.

Population : The population of the Komrem tribe is about 35,000.

Land ownership : The Komrem people are democratic nature and probably this is the reason for the non-existence of feudal system among them. There are two types of land ownership:

1) Common land which is owned by the villagers for common purpose like village reserve forest, playgrounds and grazing grounds etc.

2) *Private land* : Besides the common lands, the villagers have private lands and the individual has every right to use as the land as he likes. This right is recognised and respected by the other villagers. In the Komrem villages almost all the lands have been surveyed and given ownership rights by the Government of Manipur.

In the common land a person becomes the co-owner by virtue of being born in that village or by becoming a citizen of that village. No person other than the members of the village has the right of being the co-owner.

The individually owned land will be inherited by the male issues of the owner and in case a person has no male issue it will go to the nearest of his kins from the paternal relations. The land owned by an individual is divided equally among his male issues.

Land use System :Majority of the Komrem tribe have settled on the foothills around the Manipur valley. Most of the lands they settled in are suitable for agricultural purpose. So all the lands owned by the individuals are used for agricultural purpose, mainly for rice plantation.

Irrigation facilities are poor and non-existent in most of the lands. Hence no double-cropping is possible. The Komrem farmers should plant other crops which will help in improving their economic status.

Inheritance System : In the Komrem society women have no right of inheritance, specially in landed properties. Women can acquire but cannot inherit landed property. But some exceptions are there in case of gift and will. Women can inherit only through gift or will of the person who owned the property.

A widow can use the property of her husband only as long as she remains in the house of the husband and unmarried. A daughter is entitled to landed property if she remains unmarried throughout her life.

The clan system originated among the Komrem people as far back as the origin of the tribe itself. There are seven major clans among the Komrem tribes which were named after their ancestor's names. The clans are Leivon, Hmangte, Karong, Serto, Telien and under these major clans there are sub-clans. The clan system among the Komrem tribes is based on the ancestral names and not based on their function in thier society. The clans continued through the male issues and not through the female issues. The Komrem tribe follows patriarchal system and this is the reason why the clan continues through the male issues.

The clan system is strictly maintained and marriage is prohibited between the persons belonging to the same clan. In case a man dies intestate or without issue all his property will be inherited by his nearest clan-man. The Komrem tribes are quite closely-knit within the clans.

Inheritance and Women :As mentioned earlier, women do not remain in a particular clan to which she belongs before marriage. The Komrem society being a patriachal system only male issue continues in the clan they belong to. This being so, women have no right to inheritance to the properties of her parents unless a will has been made by her parents or she continues to be in the family without being married.

Village Council : The village council or village authority consists of some elders numbering about 7 or 8 and the chief of the village as the chairman. The members are elected by the villagers for a term which differs from village to village. Democratic system existed in the Komrem society from time immemorial. The Chiefship is however through inheritance by the male issues of the Chief. Though there is no customary law against women or female issue succeeding as chief, there is so far no instance of a woman having taken over as village chief.

Functions of Village Council : The village administration was entirely in the hands of Komrem people but with the establishment of State, the power of the village councils have been reduced to a great extent. However, the village councils still enjoy much power regarding their customary laws.

The village council decides disputes between the villagers and also disputes arising within the village. The council holds its court as and when required and it is presided by the chief of the village.

Developmental works are also taken up by the council through the funds contributed by the villagers or from the common fund acquired through common properties of the village. Government developmental works are implemented through the councils now-a-days.

One of the important functions of the village council is to maintain law and order according to their own customary laws and also to help the Government machinery. The council has different departments represented by each member of the Council.

Role of Women

In fact in the Komrem society, women are given a very respected place. She is left to herself to aspire and fulfil her own dreams. There are several women's societies which are organised and run by the women themselves among the Komrem people. In recent years women of Komrem tribes have asserted themselves in the society and their presence have been increasingly felt and seen.

Women are considered very important and are respected in the Komrem society because of the concept that it is through women that a man gets his children and formed his clan. And it is through women that his clan is expanded and developed into a society. For a Komrem husband, wife is his partner and he does not consider her as inferior.

CHAPTER V

Mao Customary Laws and Women

Mrs. Apinao Muivah

The part played by women in Mao society can be viewed mostly in and around the domestic affairs. They do not have any direct say in any of the village meetings. However we find that women play an equally important role in the family, though the father is always the head of the family. Apart from looking after the household works, caring for the children, the womenfolk also work equally hard as the menfolk in cultivation of paddy and in gardening.

At the dawn of the day the women of the house especially the mother is up and busy carrying water, fetching firewood and preparing food, so that the family members could have an early brunch and set off for the paddy fields or garden, where they spend the whole day tilting and planting vegetables or paddy. She helps her husband in digging paddy fields, jhum farms, weeding works, transplanting the rice seedlings and harvesting paddy. The mother of the house therefore is always the first to get up and the last to retire at night after finishing the household works.

Like other Naga women, Mao women are strong and active and do not find it odd to work as hard as men.

Inheritance and Women

Women have no legal rights to any kind of inheritance. Naga society permits only the males to inherit property. Mao society is also not excluded from this law. It is purely patrilineal and male ascendency is complete in it. The father is the head of the family and only the male members can inherit the family property. Females have no such right. No female is allowed to inherit the family landed property except that in some exceptional cases when landed property is given to the daughter as a marriage present. This is so in cases where the head of the family has no male issues or they happen to be a very rich family and the said landed property is not an ancestral land but acquired by father or mother at the time of marriage by their dent of labour. Besides this, the daughters have no legal share. However, daughters, till they are married, stay with their parents and enjoy their property but this privilege ceases as soon as they get married.

No ancestral land can be given to the daughters even if she happens to be the only issue. In that case the property goes to the nearest and eldest among the clansmen or they can claim it back after the death of the father if in any case the ancestral land is given to the daughters.

Widow in a Mao society is also entitled to use her husband's land and house as long as she is alive. But once she is married she has no right to her husband's property. All the property will be passed down to her sons.

In the Mao culture the youngest son inherits the house and looks after their old parents and gets a lesser share of the paddy fields, farms, woodland etc. Whereas the eldest at the time of marriage leaves his parents and constructs a new house. But he gets a larger share of the paddy fields, farms, woodland etc.

Any ancestral land is greatly valued and hardly any person will sell his share, however hard up he may become. He would prefer to borrow from others than to sell his ancestral land.

Clan System and Inheritance

A family is a small and close-knit unit. In the primitive society, when head hunting was prevalent, it was ineffective for a single family to fight against their enemies. Therefore to fight effectively against their enemies, several families would unite to form a clan. In Mao dialect clan when translated is called *Pfuta/Rezhie*. Each of these clan is traced back to a single family where the same family has multiplied into numerous families but are connected to each other, from paternal side. Such kind of two or more clans form one village.

The Head of the Clan : The clan consists of the head of the original family, the sons and the male paternal cousins. The succession to the clan headmanship will have to be always the eldest surviving son. If in any case the chief do not have a son, then he will be succeeded by his younger brother and so on.

Unlike the other Naga societies, it may be mentioned here that after the death of the king the widow of the chief can administer in the name of her minor son till he is old and able enough to assume the responsibilities as the head of the clan.

Functions and Duties of the Clan : The clan members are responsible for all the functions and duties to be performed towards each other. At the time of gatherings like feast of merit, marriage, death, plantations and harvesting of crops, all the clan members are required to come together and help one another in planning out the programmes, helping in the festivities, digging of graves and erection of memorial stones etc. Any kind of issue before it becomes the general village issue is always a clan issue first. The clan elders always gather to chalk out programmes or discuss emergency matters at regular intervals. All kinds of inter-clan disputes are brought before the village court for justice.

The members of the clan are bound by rigid rules, such as marriages with the clans are taboo and whoever breaks this taboo is excommunicated from the village. But it is also to be noted that not all gennas that broken are excommunicated but are punished in some way or the other. It depends on the type of taboo that has been violated.

There is none that does not belong to one of the clans in the Mao village. It is at the time of hardship that every individual turns to their own clan for help and moral support.

Village Council and Chieftainship

The administration of each Mao village state is carried on by a village council. Monarchical system is prevalent but at the same time it is very democratic. Each village is an independent state, the chief's court is the final court of justice and only in exceptional cases intervention may come from other village — states when their interest is adversely affected.

In the Mao society the chief possesses the right to hereditary chieftainship. He passes on the chieftainship to his eldest son but never to a daughter. But at the time of the death of the chief or oldage of the chief, if his son is still minor, then the wife/widow of the chief can administer in the name of her minor son until he attains maturity and is able to decide and act on his own. The chief is more concerned with religious rites than the administration of the village. His duty is to summon and preside over the meetings of the village council. In the administration he is assisted by the village council.

According to practice and customs, to form village council each clan in the village selects their representatives. Normally they send their eldest in the clan. They can send one to three members and the selection of their representatives would not cause any problem because according to the custom they select their own clansman basing on the seniority of the family. It may also be mentioned here that no women is selected to represent their clansman. They cannot have any direct say in the village council.

The village council is the highest body for it formulates the policy of the village. The councillors take decisions on the village welfare, make and amend the rewritten laws and they also act as judges in the highest court of the village state. It therefore enables both the wealthy as well as the poor people of the village to reach the court and sees that they are treated equally. No one is therefore ignored in any of the court cases.

The functions of the village council may be divided into three sections:-

1. Executive
2. Administrative
3. Judicial

1. *Executive*

The council has the power to punish any wrong-doer who breaks the law of the village community. There are a member of gennas observed by the society and if any villager happens to break this genna consciously or unconsciously the village council sees to it that the wrong doer is punished as befitting his mistake. No one can escape such punishment. Each and every villager is conversant with the laws and customs. Therefore, ignorance can be of no excuse.

The council also decides and settles any dispute that occurs in the village whether they be between individual or between the village and the neighbouring villages. The council decides and executes any decision as decided by them and any one who does not carry it out are punished severely.

2. *Administration*

The main administrative function of the council is to see the proper maintenance of infrastructure like road and water supply which is supposed to be one of the most important functions needed for the development of the village.

The village owned land is known as the "community land". The poor who cannot buy land of their own can utilise the community land for cultivation. This community land can also be utilised for development projects like schools, hospitals etc. with the permission from the village council.

3. *Judiciary*

Nagas on the whole love justice and the most important function of the council is judiciary. The chief and the village council constitutes the highest court of justice. All kinds of disputes and cases that arise in the village such as land dispute, fights, thefts, divorce etc. are decided and settled by this council. Criminal cases are to be decided within a time limit of 24 hours.

It is a wonder that the laws and customs practised and followed are of the past which are in practice till today. We find that only a few are amended. Mostly all laws were unwritten but they were followed as a tradition, as M. Horam describes about the judiciary system of the Nagas on the whole: "All laws are unwritten and are maintained by oral tradition. They are not flexible. On the contrary they are rigid as any written code could be".

Status of Women

It may be stated that the part played by women in the present Mao society is very limited. Most of the decisions were taken by men and she has no say at all in the social meetings. But with the coming in of Christianity, we find the women are coming up to take part in the religious meetings. Another point to be mentioned is that in the olden days, one important role played by a woman was in bringing peace between the two villages. If she does not belong to her husband's village then she can bring peace between her own village and her husband's village at the time of war. This was very much prevalent during the head hunting days. This kind of women is called *Nolo*. She is a neutral lady who acts as an ambassador in an inter-village conflict. In times of war this lady would enter the field to prevent the winner side from chasing the defeated party, thereby saving the heads of the loser. But it is to be remembered that such kind of neutral lady was not to be harmed. She was highly respected for she was related to the two villages by law and blood and was known as the symbol of peace.

CHAPTER VI

Poumai Customs

R. Vio

If we go by the Bible, we find from the very beginning, man was created first and woman was created out of his body for companionship (Gen. 2:18). God gave them equal status, equal authority to subdue and to have dominion over all other things God created. They were equally blessed and provided with the same provisions (Gen. 1:27-30). Yet at later stage particularly after the fall of man the distinction in their status came into existence: "Your desire shall be your husband and he shall rule over you" (Gen. 3:16).

Clan System

Clan means a large family group with a common ancestor. Every village consisted of three or more clans. Each clan is again divided into sub-clans on the ground of paternal origin. When a new member comes for settlement, he is attached to any of the clans whichever he chooses and accepts the authority of the first comer. The clan which settled first is honoured and respected by the late comers.

Chieftainship

Chieftainship belongs to the settler or to the selected from the clan which settled first and is handed down by heredity till the clan is extinct. The chief is the supreme head of the village affairs except in judicial affairs. He administers on the advice of the council of elders and his word carries weight. When the sowing season comes the chief fixes the time of sowing and planting. The chief first sows the seed and the villagers follow the same pattern. He can proclaim war as well as observation of religious rites. When a chief dies without male issue or during the minority of the son, his widow takes his place as the caretaker.

Any rich man hosting a feast had to give a limb of the animal killed and two tins of paddy to the chief of the village. Such a person is eligible to wear a cloth called *hasah* or *yoshosah* (white cloth) with a big horizontal stitch in the middle portion and to erect memorial of stone on the roadside to commemorate the occasion. The creation of memorial stone and the cloth signify that he is a rich man. As a token of respect the chief is given a limb of every wild beast killed.

Inheritance

1. The father is the absolute owner of all property in his possession, whether ancestral or acquired. He can deal with it in any manner he likes. Even in his lifetime he can give away some or all of his property to anybody he likes to the exclusion of all or some of his sons.

2. Daughters are excluded from inheritance of their father's property in the absence of son or sons.

3. After the death of the father, sons inherit the property. In the absence of male issue, landed property is shared by the nearest relative brothers in clan.

4. In the absence of sons, the widow succeeds to the property for her lifetime. She is not entitled to alienate that property without the knowledge of the nearest relative brother in the clan.

5. Unmarried daughter/daughters in the absence of sons and widow have interest in father's property with provision for marriage, but are not entitled to the immovable property.

6. If a widow dies intestate her property will devolve to her sons and in their absence on to the nearest relative brothers.

7. If a married daughter is divorced, she is entitled to reside at the father's house.

8. A dying father can gift to any body movable or immovable property to those who attended and served him during his sickness.

Marriage

Intermarriage is practised between clans but not in the same clan. There are two obvious forms of marriage — approved marriage and elopement. While an approved marriage is given a blessing by the parents, elopement is not blessed by the parents. Sometimes, quarrelling between families leads to fine according to the breach of customary law.

1. Approved marriage is arranged by the parents through mutual consent. If the engagement is broken either by the bride or the bridegroom, his or her marriage bond property is lost as penalty in kinds such as paddy, cow, money and so on.

2. In elopement, no marriage bond property *(heina)* is given to the boy and girl. The holy marriage ceremony should be done by the priest to join as husband and wife. The marriage should be

between members of the caste. But marriage with own sister or paternal cousin sister or clan sister is strictly prohibited. But marriage with the maternal cousin sister is allowed. The paternal cousin sister prohibition is based on the belief that when such marriage takes place, the groom will become a victim of tiger.

Divorce

Under the prevailing custom, if a husband divorces his wife, he is liable to pay his movable property to his wife. On the other hand, if the wife divorces her husband, then she loses her marriage bond property (*heina*).

If the wife is pregnant at the time of divorce, she is eligible for maintenance for the child from the husband. But if the child is grown up, he or she will go to father's house and if the child is male he will have right to inherit father's property.

CHAPTER VII

Comparative Study of Tribal Customary Laws, Manipur Land Revenue and Manipur Land Reforms Acts

Samuel Risom

Babylonian law and Nazu usage which developed around 2000 B.C. laid down that a widow did have a share in the inheritance or at least that she was to keep what she had contributed to marriage and the gifts that she had received from her husband. Elephantine contracts, the most ancient contracts, allowed a childless widow to inherit from her husband. Under the Mosaic Code, women have a right to inheritance though it had been a fundamental rule that sons alone have a right to the inheritance. Noami disposed of the properties of her deceased husband and there has been the case of Job's daughters receiving the share of inheritance along with their several brothers.

Customs are habits observed by groups of people. Self regulations of habits or conduct is a golden rule of tribal society. Customs effectively act as a mechanism for maintenance of equilibrium, social order and growth, tranquillity among the members composing the social unit and non-observance generates indignation and social wrath. Justice demands that unless there is good reason to the contrary people's hopes and aspirations are to be fulfilled. Therefore the code of justice of any legal system recognises custom as a valid rule of law.

The founding fathers of the constitution, in their wisdom, laid down that the tribals of India, especially the tribals in the North-east, will be governed by their own tribal laws. Special provisions in the constitution in Arts 224, 275 read with part III, Fifth & Sixth Schedule enshrined these rights.

As per the tribal customary laws and practices in North-east India ordinarily the inheritance of properties pass on male line - to son, if no son to brother, and if no brother to nearest relative. Except tribes like Garo, Khasi where the matrilineal rule is followed, both patrilineal primogeniture and patrilineal ultimogeniture rule of inheritance are followed. Even among the tribals who follow the rule of patrilineal inheritance, there is no express bar against the inheritance of properties by the female members as the father who is the absolute owner of paternal properties, often gifts away paternal properties to daughters at the time of their marriage or during father's life-time.

The Tripuris follow neither the rule of primogeniture nor ultimogeniture. On marriage father gives away such shares he sets apart and whoever looks after the aged parents till death takes the share of property kept by the father for himself. Father can also deny the share of inheritance to any prospective heir.

Some of the cases are discussed here for deeper understanding of the tribal customary practices - I.D. Barma of Brahmacherra village inherited all the paternal properties to the exclusion of his three brothers as he commanded the confidence of his father. Later he gave away his sisters in marriage and distributed equal shares of paternal properties to his elder and younger brothers. Two sons of Mr A, namely Amarandra and Ajoy of the same village, were not given landed property by their father though their mother and sister Satyabari received their shares of landed properties. The reasons for denial were that first son, Amarandra was disobedient and Ajoy was too young at the time of father's death.

Shri Vidyamohan being unable to meet family expenditure sold a plot of land without consulting his wife. Unable to resist her temper, she assaulted her husband. It is not customary to assault husband without first placing the matter before the Village Council and accordingly she was fined Rs 5 and a bottle of wine by the Village Council.

The Apatanis, the Adis of Arunachal Pradesh also ignore the female line while passing on the properties and are strictly patriarchal society. But often, daughters are entitled to inherit the father's self-acquired properties if she had looked after her father in his old age or sacrifices a mithun after her father's death for father's funeral ceremony. Otherwise also, father can gift away his properties to daughters without any customary inhibition.

Some cases of Apatani society are discussed here. Apatanis follow the principle of patriarchal primogeniture. Sons and daughters leave parental house after marriage. All family members are normally consulted for taking important decisions. Ordinarily widows have no right to dispose of family property and daughters are excluded from inheritance. Hage Pulo of Hari village gave all properties to his two daughters since there was no male issue. Shri Gyati Tasar distributed the whole family properties to his daughters Miss Tane and Miss Yapia. In these two cases, the daughters looked after the aged parents till death and sacrificed mithun after father's death for funeral ceremonies.

Jamatias in Tripura inherit properties in equal shares by the daughters in the absence of male issues though the system of inheritance is patrilineal. The Halams too follow the system of patrilineal but often times father gifts away properties to his daughters without any objection from prospective heirs. The Reangs follow rules of patrilineal inheritance. All the sons in the family equally share the properties left by the father. Normally daughters were given shares by the father during his life-time.

The Lushais follow the rule of patrilineal ultimogeniture like Rongmeis, Chakhesangs etc. Father is the absolute authority and may even deprive prospective heir if he so wishes. Very often daughters were given share of the landed properties.

In Civil Revision No. 11(h) of 1971, the Gauhati High court held that Miss Laldingpui was entitled to inherit the property of her aunt with whom she had lived and helped in all possible manner from her childhood. In this case the aunt had not expressly nominated Miss Laldingpui to be her heir but the fact of their living together gave enough ground for valid presumption as heir.

According to the Chakhesang practices, the properties which are given to daughters by the father as gifts become the absolute property of the women and such type of properties are strictly passed on the female line, and the male members in the family have no claim over such property.

The Garo society is basically matrilineal and inheritance is through the female line from mother to daughter. Daughters claim to inherit properties according to their customary laws and usages was upheld by the Gauhati High Court in Civil Revision No. 12 (H) of 1975. In Garo society male members in the family retains the right of maintenance and help manage the properties.

Almost all other tribal societies in the North-east follow the same kind of tradition and often daughters are used to get shares of paternal properties along with the sons because while the father was setting his house in order before his death felt proper to distribute properties so that no one suffered after him. Father enjoyed absolute authority over his properties and had the power of disposal in any manner in conformity with customary inheritance, that is to say, whenever father gifts away his property to daughters during his lifetime no other prospective heir shall have claim over it.

Village Council : Ordinarily the village council members are selected from the older members of the clans who are wise, honest, influential and knowledgeable. Council members project the image of the village and its honour. There was express bar against women's participation in the village council. There had been occasions in the history of Tangkhul when women had become members of the Village Council and represented the spokesperson of the village for a very simple reason that those women had better knowledge of language and conversation.

Land Use System : The concept of all land belonging to the Pharaoh in Egypt or the doctrine of King's land do not apply to the tribals. The doctrine says that in the whole world, there is no land which is not the King's land. In these tribal societies, the communities, families and individuals had their own lands which the King could acquire only by purchase from the owners. There are three ways of acquiring land rights - inheritance from the previous owner, transfer from previous owner and by way of reclaiming new site within the community land. Now-a-days, government also allots land to individuals from government land.

Tribals considered land as a living thing superior to human life and therefore any person falsely claiming land risked his life. For the guilty person the earth which desolves in water becomes a water of bitterness and cursing which ultimately causes death.

The Manipur Land Revenue and Land Reforms Act 1960 (hereinafter as MLR) is not extended to the Hill Areas of Manipur. But there is a proviso that the State Government may extend it to any part of the Hill Areas if deemed proper.

Section 11 of the Act declares that all lands including forest, mines and minerals which are not the property of any person are the property of the state. It is to be stated that in the Hill areas or villages there is no land which is not the property of any person. The land in the villages are either individually owned or collectively owned by the villagers. Under MLR, the owners of land liable to pay revenue are given *patta* signed by the Deputy Commissioner which recognised the rights of the land covered by the *patta* and this right is heritable and transferable. Both men and women can obtain *patta* (land allotment) from the Deputy Commissioner.

Under MLR, the landholding of a family is limited to 10 hectares in case of non-irrigated land, and less than 10 for irrigated land. Except a few cases, all persons having *patta* land have to pay land revenue according to the value and nature of the land utilised. Under MLR, there is a provision which prohibits transfer of a tribal's land to a non-tribal without the previous permission of the Deputy Commissioner and the consent of the concerned District Council and any transfer of rights without fulfilling this provision will render the right forfeited to the previous owner.

In the Hill Areas, a Hill House Tax of Rs 6 is collected from every household in lieu of land revenue but in many pockets of hill villages, both Land Revenue and Hill House Tax are being collected in violation of law. This collection of double taxation from the Hill People had been constantly brought to the attention of the State Government. The Law Department also had advised the abolition of double taxation (see the minutes of the meeting of the Deputy Commissioners dt. 15.9.1983).

The rate of House Tax in Manipur is very high. In Arunachal Pradesh the rate of annual house-tax is Rs 2. In Garo Hills it is Rs 3.95 per household. In Manipur it is Rs 6 since 1975 and it is further proposed to be raised to Rs 10 which would weigh heavy on the tribals.

Much has been talked about the extension of MLR in the Hill Areas of Manipur by the Government with the support of the Maiteis, the majority community. I am not saying anything on this count other than quoting what J.N.Das, Director, Study of Land System, Law Research Institute, Gauhati High Court has written in the preface of the book entitled, *A Study of the Land System of North Eastern Region Vol.V-Manipur (1985)*:- "We have made our observation to the effect that there need be no hurry to extend the provisions of the Act to the hill-districts in a general way".

Lastly, it has to be mentioned that in the Hill Districts where the Naga and the Kuki groups live, the land system is regulated entirely by perennial customs.

CHAPTER VIII

Clan System of the Vaipheis

Rev. S. Prim Vaiphei

According to the tradition of the Vaipheis, Manmasi was the first man on earth. Like Adam in the Bible, he is sometimes identified with human being. Zahong was one of the descendants of Manmasi. Zahong once lived under the earth and Nuaimangpa was the king of this subterranean world. One day Nuaimangpa conducted the *chon* feast and all his subjects were in the feast. In the feast, *Thankip* (chameleon) was the drumer and *uphok* (frog) was the steward of the feast.

In this feast all the youths contested in high jump, jumping over the mithun which was to be killed for the feast. But no one could jump over successfully. Zahong did not join the high jump, he was doing the work of *nangmet* (cutting bamboo into pieces for binding things). The people called Zahong to join the high jump contest. Zahong then hanged his sword under his shoulder and covered it with his shawl. However when he ran for the high jump, he hurt one pregnant woman (who was watching the game) with his sword and she died. Zahong felt so sad and shy. He therefore, decided to leave the subterranean world. He thus came out through a cave known *as khul* along with his colleagues. But the gate of the *khul* was closed by a big stone and a big serpent called *gulheupi* was on the side of the stone.

Vangalpa, one of the colleagues of Zahong lifted up the stone and Zahong covered his head with a thick cloth called *phoipi*. He folded the cloth into seven fold, covered his head and put his sharp sword (machette) over the cloth. Thus he came out of the *khul*. And when the serpent fell upon him, it hit the sharp sword and was cut into three pieces. It was because he opened the gate of the cave for many, he was called Zahong (za - many; hong -open = open for many). It is because of this, when his descendants kill an enemy or tiger, they shout/chant what is called *hanla* (song of the brave) saying "Kathange kathange, khulsin dongkot kahonge" which means "I am famous, I am famous, I opened the gate of the *khul*". Here the one who shouts *hanla* is identified himself with his ancestor Zahong and says " I open the gate of the cave".

There are different versions about this. According to some traditions, it was Sattong one of the descendants of Zahong, who came out of the *khul*. Some Suantaks (descendants of Suantak) claim that it was Suantak who came out of the cave.

Some people identified this Zahong with Hangmi and say that Zahong and Hangmi are the different names of one person. Hangmi is another name of Zahong. However in another version, Hangmi was the brother of Hangtak, Hangba and Hangsuan. Again, another version says that Tualzumang the father of Zahong was the one who came out of the *khul*. According to this version, Tualzumang named his son Zahong because he opened the gate of the cave. The descendants of Hangmi identified their progenitor Hangmi with Zahong, the descendants of Suantak identified their progenitor Suantak with Zahong. But it is commonly agreed that Zahong was the one who came out of the *khul*.

After they came out of the *khul*, they lived at a place called *khuasinlung*. While they were there, there came a great darkness which lasted for seven days and seven nights. Tradition says that this darkness called *thimzin* caused much trouble to the people. The people who felt asleep turned into beasts, stones and trees. Pu Zahong's family had a great stock of skulls of animals and of foes which they could use as fuel for fire during the period of darkness. They propped open their eyes with pieces of bamboo and danced throughout the period of darkness beating their drums. We do not know when this darkness (thimzin) happened. Some say, it was during the time of Zahong and some say, it was during the time of Suantak. Many blindly identify Suantak with Zahong.

The Vaipheis also have a story of a great flood known as *tuitawbin*. This flood is also sometimes associated with the *thimzin*. It is said that during this flood all the living beings took shelter at *Khawlkipzang* also known as *mitinbung*. Whenever a person is bitten by an animal like bear, boar, tiger etc., they offered sacrifice for the healing of the wounded person and the priest (*thiampu*) muttered his charm saying "my female tiger, my male tiger, you have been friend with human beings ... during the flood, men and animals lived together at *mitinbung* and God asked us not to harm each other ... my male tiger, my female tiger you have wronged first ... let the spot/mark hurt by your nail, by your teeth be healed". It is said that the flood was because *thangnel* (water god) fell in love with a human girl, the daughter of Lianthang. And thus when the people threw the girl into the water, the flood receded. When this flood came, all people lived together with the beast at *khawlkipzang*. They were friendly and lived together in peace. However oneday a tiger killed a pregnant woman Ngainu by name and removed the child from her womb. That was the beginning of the enmity between men and animals.

According to the tradition of the Meitei, Manipur valley was once covered by water. The flood was drained out by the gods who made it possible for people to live in the valley. Some say that this story of the Meiteis is the same incident as of *tuitawbin*.

Besides, tiger also killed the mithun of Tusing (progenitor of the Buites) and stole the eggs of a widow and the widow threw her wodden load upon the tiger and killed it. This was the beginning of enmity between men and animals.

The name Vaiphei

There was a time when all the tribes lived together at one place. The place was known as *Khuavaiphei*. This *khuavaiphei* is also identified with *khawlkipzang*. There is a clear evidence that all tribes, people of various clans lived together at *khuavaiphei.* Whenever the ancestors killed a big animal or enemy, they used to shout or chant what they called *hanla* (meaning song of the brave"). The songs goes like this "I am renowned, I am famous, since I was born from *khul*, my parents praise me, in the village of Vaiphei, a village of many tribes and race, I am famous".

Later on they moved out from *khuavaiphei*, tribe by tribe and clan by clan to different directions. The group which left *khuavaiphei* first were the *Paites.* For this reason they are known as *Paites* means those who have gone. The group which went to the south came to be known as Simtes (southerners). Those who have gone to the western side came to be known as Khuathang (westerner). They are now known as Hmar (means northerners) because they lived on northern side of the Luseis. Those who went to the cold hill regions came to be known as *Jous*. Among the Thadous, the Haokips went to the eastern side and thus they were known as *khuasakte*. Thus the group which remained at *khuavaiphei* later came to be known as Vaipheis. The clans (or part of the clans) who remained at khuavaiphei and later came to be known as *Vaipheis* are Suantaks, Chonlu, Khautes, Buites, Neihsials, Neithams, Singphuns, Ngoilus, Chulzangs, Singphuns, Dulians, Hawinge, Haulais, etc.

Being the head of the clans and the chief of the region, Suantaks' families collected *samal changseu* (tax of paddy and meat, i.e. the right hind leg of animals killed by whatsoever means) from the subjects. As a result of this even in the later time, the village chiefs who collected tax of *samal changseu* from the villagers use to say "Suantakpa nek ah kane" means "I take it was Suantak does". When a person died in an accident, the priest went to the spot of accident and performed a ceremony known as *tualthiak* (means cleansing the ground). Here the priest muttered his charms asking the soul of the person who died in the accident, not to stay there in the jungle but to return home saying: "go to your living village, you should not stay here in the wilderness, I am cleaning the ground as Suantak did from time of the past."

Whenever the Vaipheis offered a sacrifice known as *Akthiam kithawi*, the priest muttered his charms saying "go to the village of Suantak with your sacrificial materials, the plate of vawng wood and the torch of palm wood". These are done by all Vaipheis.

Some people identified this *khuavaiphei* with Phaiza, a village of the Vaipheis in Chinhills. It is true that the people who are now known as Vaipheis lived at Phaiza. But all of them did not live at Phaiza. Phaiza was the village of the Suantaks and the Lutngul clan was the chief of the village. Contemporary Vaiphei villages with Phaiza are Sipi (the village of Thangniang clan) Sialkal (the village of Hansing clan), Hiangpek (the village of Thanglet clan), Saiva (the village of Tusing/Buite clan), Thalmual (the village of Neitham, Khuazim, Khuabual, Zooupi (the villages of Khautes). After the defeat of Phaiza at the hands of the enemies, some families from Lutngul clan set up another village known as Haimual.

Since they moved towards different directions and lived in different places, their languages also became different from each other. Dr. Vumkhohau rightly says: "On account of difficult communication in the regions inhabited by the Zo race, contacts between communities were infrequent and as a result the formerly unified language spoken by a single race tended to split into a variety of dialects (Zo Suan Khang Simna Laibu foreword page iii).

As we are the people who do not have written record about our origin and clan, there are different versions and theories about our origins. There are much discrepencies on our geneological tree.

According to the people of Chinhills, the first man (human being) was Zou. The sons of Zou were Kipmang and Cinhil. The son of Kipmang was Nawphut. The son of Nawphut was Nawsong. Nawsong and was the father of Chongthu/Songthu. Songthu was the father of Sungmang, Sungmang was the father of Songkip, Songza, Zakhai and Zahong. Songkip was the progenitor of Nongchom, Akgal, Manlun, Manchuang, Mangson, Hangvung, Matmang. Songza was the progenitor of Mate, Hehthang, Langsun, Langen. Zahong was the progenitor of Thadous, Suantaks (Vaipheis). According to them, Sektak/Sehtha, the progenitor of the Thadous and Suantak were brothers.

However, according to the version of the Thadous and the Suantaks in Manipur, Songthu/Chongthu is the progenitor of Titou (Doungels), Touhin (Thadous), Touthang (Lamhaus). Zahong is the progenitor of the Vaipheis and the Gangtes. The chart I make here is according to the theory of our ancestors in Manipur. Clan and geneological tree follows male line. Woman have no place in the genealogical line.

According to one theory, Phullum was the progenitor of Khautes and Lunglum. The progenitors of Hualngous were the younger brothers of Lianlut. Lianlut had two sons - Sattong (the progenitor of the Suantaks) and Thanglun (the progenitor of the Gangtes). However, according to another theory, Tongbul the son of Sattong had two sons Liankhup and Chonning. Chonning was the father of Tusing and Tusing was the progenitor of Buites, Singphuns and Neitham. Liankhup (who is also identified with Suanpau by some people) had five sons - Thailo, Hangtak, Hangba, Hangsuan and Hangmi. Thailo died without having a son. Hangtak was the progenitor of the Suantaks, Hangba of the Chungnung/Tungnung and Tongdium, Hangsuan of the Khautes and Hangmi of the Ngoilus and Mihrem.

We do not know when the Suantak line and the Khaute line were separated. Some say, it was from the time of Lianlut, as cited above. Another theory which is more acceptable is that Hangtak, Hangba, Hangsuan and Hangmi were brothers. Hangtak was the progenitor of Suantak clan, Hangba or Tungnung and Tungdium of Hangsuan of Khautes and Hangmi of Buites, Ngoilu and Mihrems. Some Khautes claim that Buite is the junior clan (naupa) of Khaute. But the Buites do not accept this. Hangmi had two sons Chonhau (the progenitor of Ngailu, Lupho, Lupheng and Misao) and Chonning (the progenitor of Buites, Singphuns, Nungan and Neihtham). The Buites claim that the Ngoilu and the Mihrem are the junior clan *(naupa)* of Buite. But the later do not accept this. We do not know who was the elder one between Chonning and Chonhau. The Ngoilus maintain that they are the *naupa* (junior clan) of Sauntak and the Sauntaks also accept this.

It is said that Ngailu, a kinsman of Suantak was in Chinhills. He accidentally killed a man and in order to escape the reaction, he came to Manipur. When he came to Manipur, he told the people that he was from Suantak clan. The Haokips, who did not know his true identity did not believe him to be from Suantak clan and sang a song like this "the one who was Ngoilu in the beginning and now claim to be Suantak - if you are looking for a high clan, don't you see Doungul and Song that is'? In reply, Ngoilu sang: " I claim that I am Suantak not because I am looking for a high class clan, I Ngoilu Suantak am as high as I am". It is said that when the Suantak came to Manipur in the time of Mangzalut and lived at Natok, the Ngoilus came to him to revive the old relation and gave *sating* and these acknowledged that Suantak was his *upa* (senior clan). Whoever may be the elder one between the Ngoilu and the Buite, they are the junior clans of Suantak; and tradition, sorcery/charm (*doithu*) confirms that Neitham was the youngest among the Vaipheis.

Tradition says that Suantak once visited his friend Manlun, whose wife was barren. Suantak slept with that barren woman, the wife of his friend Manlun. The barren woman bore a son (with Suantak) and his name was Gegu (Ngengu). When Manlun discovered that the child of his wife was not his, he disowned his wife. Suantak took her to be his wife and she bore more sons and daughers.

Suantak, the elder brother of Khuakuan (Paute) had other sons with his legitimate wife and they were Neilut, Tomsoi and Thansoi (Luangte). Neilut did not love Thangsoi, because of this Thangsoi sang a song "Neilut hates me and separates me". Thangsoi set up his own village at Luangmual. From there, he came to be known as Luangte.

Khuakuan/Paute set up his own village at Chongtui and then Tuisim. While he was at Tuisim he could not protect his village from the enemies. He therefore invited Mangvung one of the sons of Haokip to protect his village. Because of this the descendants of Khuakuan (the Baites) lived among the Mangvung Haokips and adopted Haokip customs and culture.

Luangte, while he was at Buangmual reared a wild boar and the boar killed his wife who was pregnant. Luangte lamented "I kept a boar in a den and this made me lose my wife."

We do not know which among the different theories is the most correct one and authoritative. However, though there are various theories and versions - all agree that Suantaks, Khautes, Ngailus, Mihrems, Buites, Singphun, Dulians, Neihsials, Neihthams etc. are from one family. Among the Thadous, the Haokips forgot that they are the descendants of the Thadou. So also, the Thangniangs, Thangluais and Sialiaps forgot that they are the descendants of Suantak, and they disown the name Suantak. The Suantes and Khupmu also forgot that they are within Suantak clan.

The Death of Suantak

Suantak was the king of Phaiza. His sons Gegu (Ngengu), Daitong and Vanglok were at Sizang. But Neilut, Tomsoi and Thangsois were at Phaiza. All the people of the region gave tribute to Suantak. One day a man from Thanglun (Gangte) clan killed one deer (Sazuk) and brought him a right hind leg of the animal he killed. When Suantak saw it, he asked the man saying "why don't you bring a knife to cut the meat, a basket to keep it and a *tul* (pointed iron rod used to dry meat) to hang the meat". When the man saw that Suantak was too proud, he was so angry that he hit the head of Suantak with the leg of the animal, three times saying "This is the knife, this is the basket, this is the *tul* and thus killed Suantak. Because of this, the Thanglun families could not stay there at Phaiza and migrated to a place called Gangmun and thus they came to be known as Gangtes. Though the relationship between the Suantaks and the Gangtes was broken because of this, many elderly people do not forget that the Gangtes are the junior brothers *(naupa)* of the Suantaks.

In the early 20th century, sometimes in the early 1910s, there was a quarrel between the Gangtes and the Singsuans. The trouble started from Suangsang village in the time of Nungkhogin. The Gangtes were in trouble and appealed to the people of Suantak that " you are our *upa* (senior clan) and now save us from the hands of our enemies". The Suantaks collected money (1/4 of a rupee=siki) from among themselves and killed one pig for peace negotiation and made them compromise. Late Nungkholian of Mintha (Phaizang) came to Manamzang village and requested the Suantak family for help. Later Mr. Neikhothang (Kaikhopa) went among the Baites for the said collection of money. The amount they collected was Rs. 200/-.

While our forefathers lived in Chinhills, once there was a war between the Thadous and the Vaipheis. The Vaipheis were very proud and said with a haugty spirit "can we not combine killing the Thadous with smoking tobacco pipe?'. In the war the spirit (demons) of Lunglen took the side of the Sitlhous (Thadous). It is said that the Zampi village (Of the Thadous) and the demons of Lunglen were friends. The Singsuans of Tuithang and the Khuangzang villages, the *naupa* (junior clan) of the Sitlhous also sided the Sitlhous. The Vaipheis were defeated in the war. They surrendered to the Thadous and gave the ivory of Sipi known as *Sipite saiha* and the Thangniang dak (the gong of Thangniang) to the Thadous as peace negotiation gifts. After this defeat, the Vaipheis became very weak and could not live at Phaiza because of the frequent attack of the Pois. Thus the Lutnguls (the chief family of Phaiza) shifted to Haimual and settled there. This village was also defeated by the Pois and thus the Vaipheis came to Manipur.

The sequential order of Suantak villages from before the time of Suantak were - from Khuasinlung to Khuamaupi, from Khuamaupi to Khuazawlpi, from Khuazawlpi to Thingthak, from Thingthak to Inbuk, from Inbuk to Chaimnuaikhua, from Chimnuaikhua to Geltui, from Geltui to Khawlkipzang, from Khawlkipzang to Pilou, from Pilou to Louzang, from Louzang to Hiangpek, from Hiangpek to Phaiza. From Phaiza, the Thanglet family (head of Suantak clan) moved to Changtui, then to Suangpilon, then to Hakak, then to Mualngat, then to Leisan, then to Maokot, then to Tongkholon, then to Khiangte, then to Mazulon, then to Salam, then to Phailengzang, then to Khuanglo, then to Mauzang, then to Karakhun, then to Khualipok (Manamzang), then to Langmaiching. Now the sons of Zamkhothang (Head of Suantak clan) live at Langmaiching.

Some contend that the chief of Phaiza was the Thanglet (head of the clan), while others contend that Leisel family was the chief of Phaiza. These are not true. The Thanglet had their own village at Hiangpek and due to the frequent attack of the enemies they moved to Phaiza, the village of the Lutngul and then to Changtui. We have come across to another Changtui, a village of the Baite clan. We do not know whether this Chongtui of the Baite is the same with the Changtui of Thanglet family or a different one which is more probable.

The Chief of Phaiza was the Lutngul family. Pu Tuinoi (a descendant of Lutngul) had a *chon* feast at Phaiza because he was the king of the region. His two sons Tinsum and Mangkhopau were heroes of Phaiza.

During their reign, they defeated many foes and they took *chelthil* from the people of Phaium/Phailum after defeating them. Chelthil is a valuable object taken as tribute from the said tribe. There is a song of the Lutngul about this Chelthil. "My chelthil though valuable but can not speak'".

During their reign at Phaiza, Sialliap were used as *Tangsam* (the one who shout for giving information to the villagers), and Buites were as *thiempu* (priest). My great grandfather Lutzangul was known as 'Phaiza galhatpa'(hero of Phaiza). Being the king, the Lutngul king cooked the pigs without cutting into pieces. That is why there is a saying "Lutngul vawktawndawn" means Lutngul who holds pig without being dressed. The Lutngul families killed number of pigs without cutting the flesh into pieces as a sign of honour and richness.

Sauntaks and the Khautes

In the Chinhills, Myanmar, the Khautes, Vangluas are included within Suantak clan.

Suantak covers them too. But herein Manipur, the Khautes disown Suantak. Some of them even claim to be the *upa* (senior clan) of Suantak and many admit that the Khaute is the junior clan to Suantak. There was a dispute over this seniority of the clan between the Suantaks and the Khautes in the early 1940s. They challenged each other for diving in order to decide whose clan was the senior one. The Suantak clan was represented by a man from S. Kotlian and the Khaute clan was represented by a man from K. Kawtlian. The date and the hour for the diving was set, but later they dropped the plan. We do not know when the two brothers were seperated. Though some Khautes contend like this in a song known as Tinbuk lapi (the song of Tinbuk) that Khaute is junior to Suantak. The song goes "though I am the youngest in the clan, I am above all others". This shows that he was rich and strong in the village than any other person of his time.

Not only the Khautes, the Baites also claim that they are above Suantaks, a senior clan of Suantak. So also Mihrem, Lupho and Lupheng claim that they are senior clan to Suantak, but Ngoilu, the upa (senior clan) of the Lupho and Lupheng already admit that they are the *naupa* (junior clan) of Suantak. The Thadous, the Chongthus/Songthus also claim that they are above Suantak, senior to Suantak. However, the Suantak acknowledge none of these calims. The Suantaks contend that Suantak clan is the head (senior clan) of all clans.

I do not claim that the information and the chart I give here are the most correct. These are according to the information I received from various sources. Since there are various theories and versions, we do not know which one shall be the most correct one. I include here the theories and versions which are accepted by the majority.

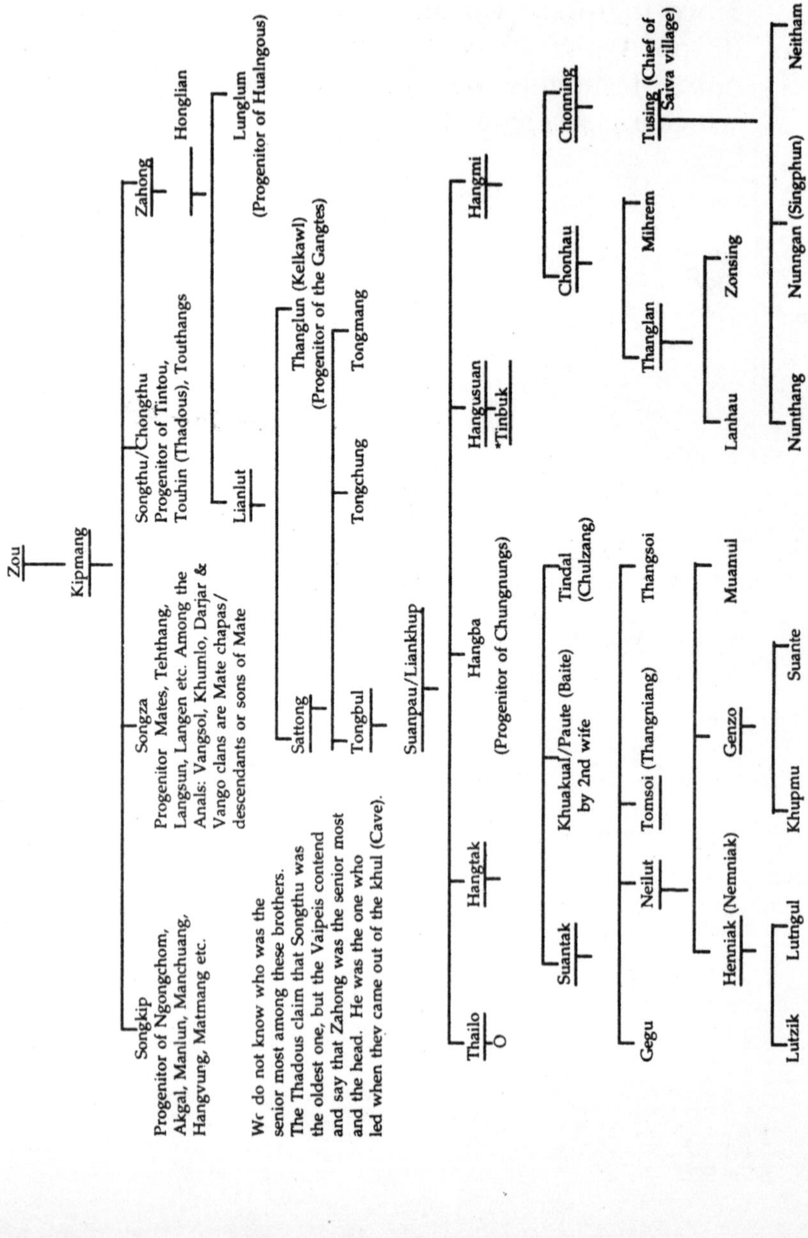
Zou
Kipmang
Songkip
Progenitor of Ngongchom, Akgal, Manlun, Manchuang, Hangvung, Matmang etc.
Songza
Progenitor Mates, Tehthang, Langsun, Langen etc. Among the Anals: Vangsol, Khumlo, Darjar & Vango clans are Mate chapas/ descendants or sons of Mate
Songthu/Chongthu
Progenitor of Tintou, Touhin (Thadous), Touthangs
Zahong
Honglian
Lianlut
Lunglum
(Progenitor of Hualngous)
We do not know who was the senior most among these brothers. The Thadous claim that Songthu was the oldest one, but the Vaipeis contend and say that Zahong was the senior most and the head. He was the one who led when they came out of the khul (Cave).
Sattong
Thanglun (Kelkawl)
(Progenitor of the Gangtes)
Tongbul
Tongchung
Tongmang
Suanpau/Liankhup
Thailo
Hangtak
Hangba
(Progenitor of Chungnungs)
Hangusuan
*Tinbuk
Hangmi
Suantak
Khuakual/Paute (Baite)
by 2nd wife
Tindal
(Chulzang)
Chonhau
Chonning
Gegu
Neilut
Tomsoi (Thangniang)
Thangsoi
Thanglan
Mihrem
Tusing (Chief of Saiva village)
Henniak (Nemniak)
Genzo
Muamul
Lanhau
Zonsing
Lutzik
Lutngul
Khupmu
Suante
Nunthang
Nunngan (Singphun)
Neitham

Suantak once visited his friend Manlun whose wife was barren.. The wife invited Suantak to sleep with her, because she wanted to have a child. Suantak consented. The woman became pregnant & bore a male child. His name was Gegu (Ngengu). He was born younger to Neilut.
We do not know who was the older one between Chonhau & Chonning.

Dolbuk

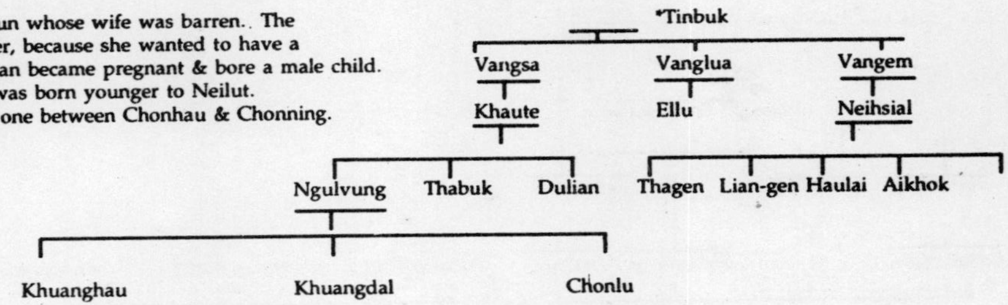

It is said that Vangsa was suffering from leprosy. So his descendants prefered to bear the name of his younger brother Vanglua .

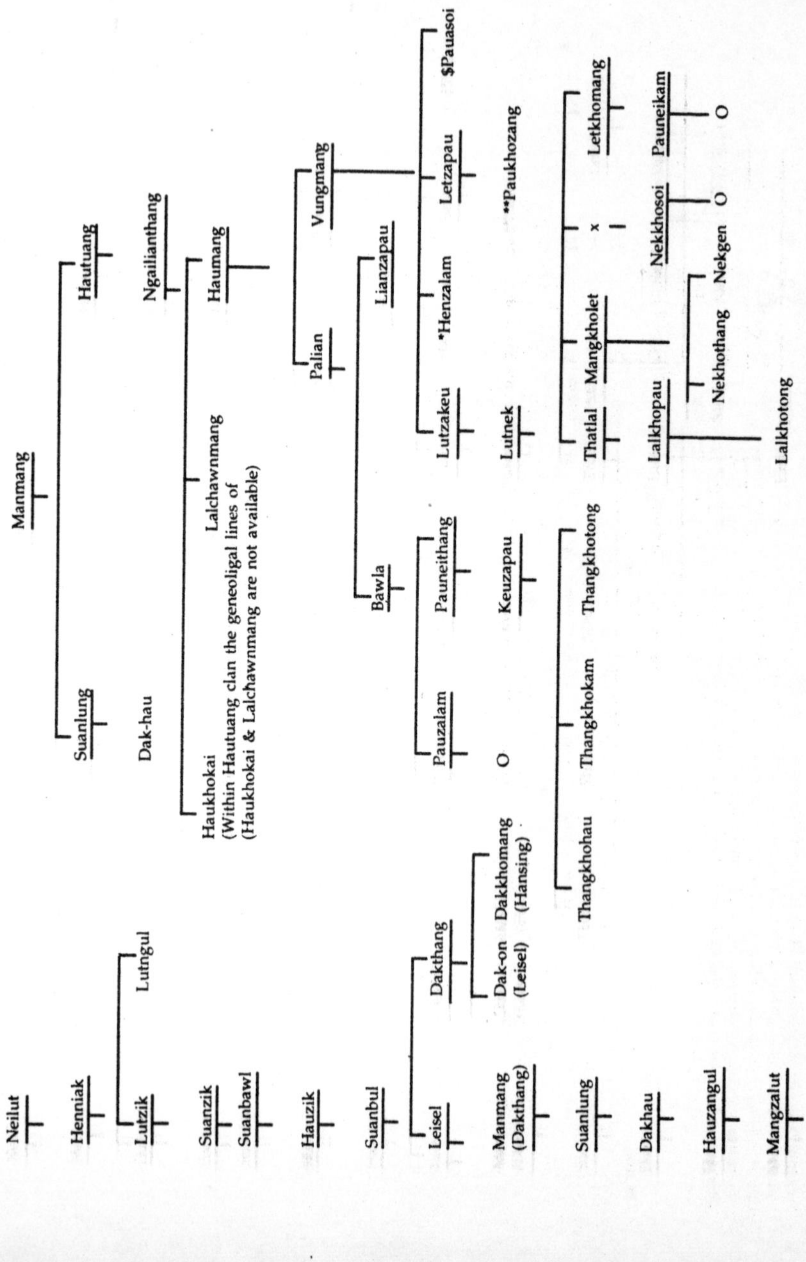
Neilut
Henniak
Lutzik
Lutngul
Suanzik
Suanbawl
Hauzik
Suanbul
Leisel
Dakthang
Dak-on (Leisel)
Dakkhomang (Hansing)
Manmang (Dakthang)
Suanlung
Dakhau
Hauzangul
Mangzalut
Manmang
Suanlung
Hautuang
Dak-hau
Ngailianthang
Haukhokai
Lalchawnmang
Haumang
(Within Hautuang clan the geneoligal lines of
(Haukhokai & Lalchawnmang are not available)
Palian
Vungmang
Bawla
Lianzapau
Pauzalam
Pauneithang
O
Keuzapau
Lutzakeu
*Henzalam
Letzapau
$Pauasoi
Lutnek
**Paukhozang
Thangkhohau
Thangkhokam
Thangkhotong
Thatlal
Mangkholet
x
Letkhomang
Lalkhopau
Nekhothang
Nekgen
Nekkhosoi
O
Pauneikam
O
Lalkhotong

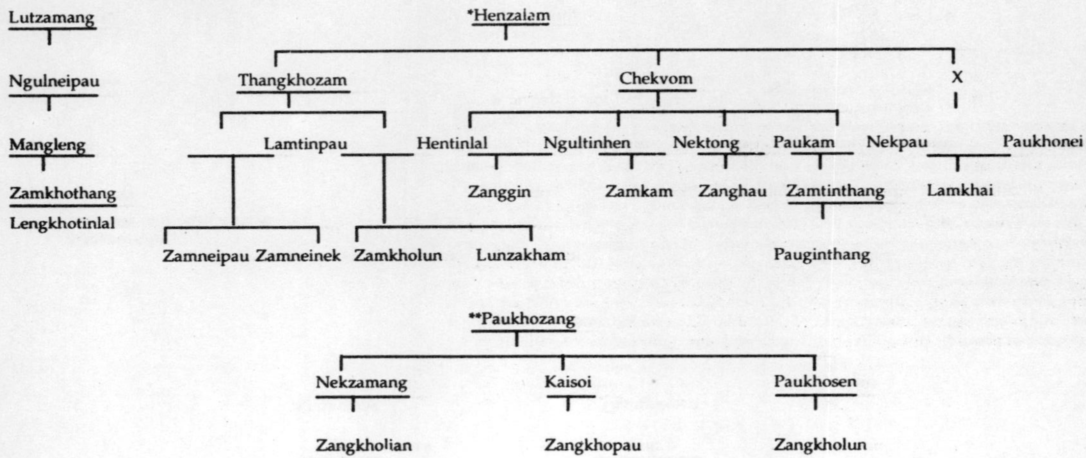

This Lengkhotinlal's line is the head of Suantak clan. Now the descendants of Gegu (Ngengu) contend that Gegu was older than Neilut, but if Gegu was the older one, when Tuinoi (Lutngul) performed the *chon* feast, he could have invited his descendant to kill the mithun. The fact he (Tuinoi) invited Leisel who later came to be known as Thanglet, shows that there was no one senior to him. Tuinoi invited Thanglet because of his birthright.

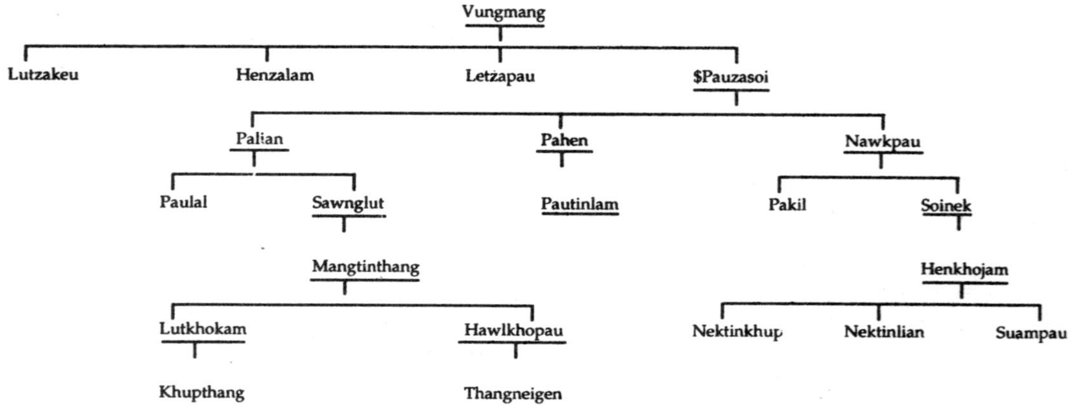

Approved by:
Thangkhohau, Saram Patawng

Pu Lutngul's descendant pu Tuinol had a *chon* festival. In this festival the head of the clan should kill the mithun thrusting a sharp point iron rod called *chontul* on the side of the game (mithun). So he invited pu Leisel (the head of the clan) for this, but Leisel did not turn up on time. So Dakthang who was next to him killed the mithun. When Leisel arrived the mithun was killed by Dakthang. He was so unhappy and thus gave his name Leisel to Dakthang and he himself took the name Dakthang. After sometime he killed one boar and he shouted what they called *hanla* saying "Dakthang pan kathang talet e" (I Dakthang am famous now). From this time onward, he and his family came to be known as *Thanglet*. So within the clan of Thanglet *Manmang* is the head and next to Manmang is *Hautuang* (the geneological tree of Hautuang is not included here because it is not available). Next to Hautuang is Haumang and Haumang's next is Hanngul. Next to this comes the sub-clan of Leisel (who was known as Dakthang). Leisel's younger brother is Hansing. The geneological tree of Hansing sub-clan is not available and thus not included here in the chart. So also the geneological tree of Sialiap is not included in the Chart. (It is not available).

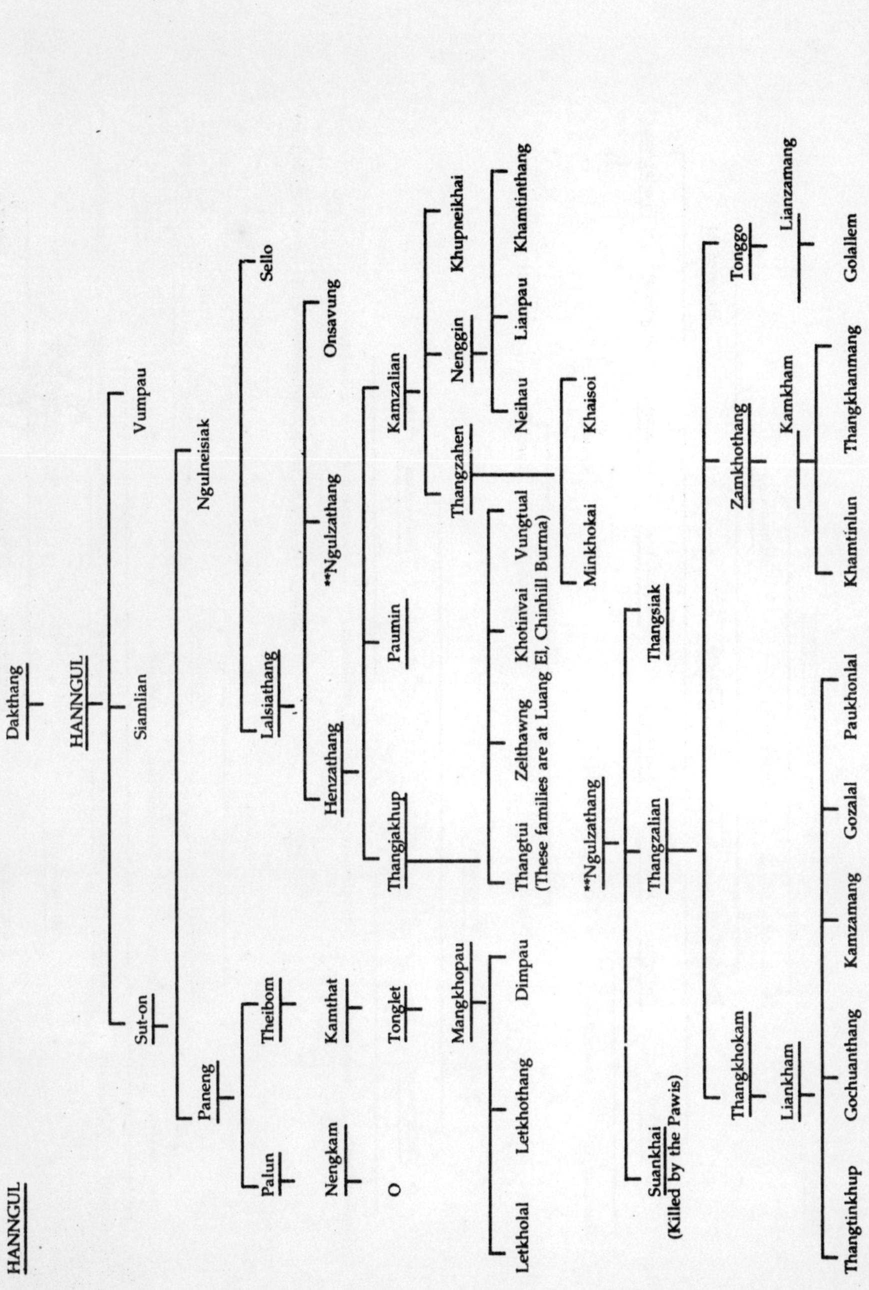
HANNGUL
Dakthang
HANNGUL
Sut-on
Siamlian
Vumpau
Paneng
Ngulneisiak
Palun
Theibom
Lalsiathang
Sello
Nengkam
Kamthat
Henzathang
**Ngulzathang
Onsavung
O
Tonglet
Thangjakhup
Paumin
Kamzalian
Mangkhopau
Thangzahen
Nenggin
Khupneikhai
Letkholal
Letkhothang
Dimpau
Thangtui
Zelthawng
Khotinvai
Vungtual
Neihau
Lianpau
Khamtinthang
(These families are at Luang El, Chinhill Burma)
Minkhokai
Khaisoi
**Ngulzathang
Suankhai
(Killed by the Pawis)
Thangzalian
Thangsiak
Thangkhokam
Zamkhothang
Tonggo
Liankham
Kamkham
Lianzamang
Thangtinkhup
Gochuanthang
Kamzamang
Gozalal
Paukhonlal
Khamtinlun
Thangkhanmang
Golallem

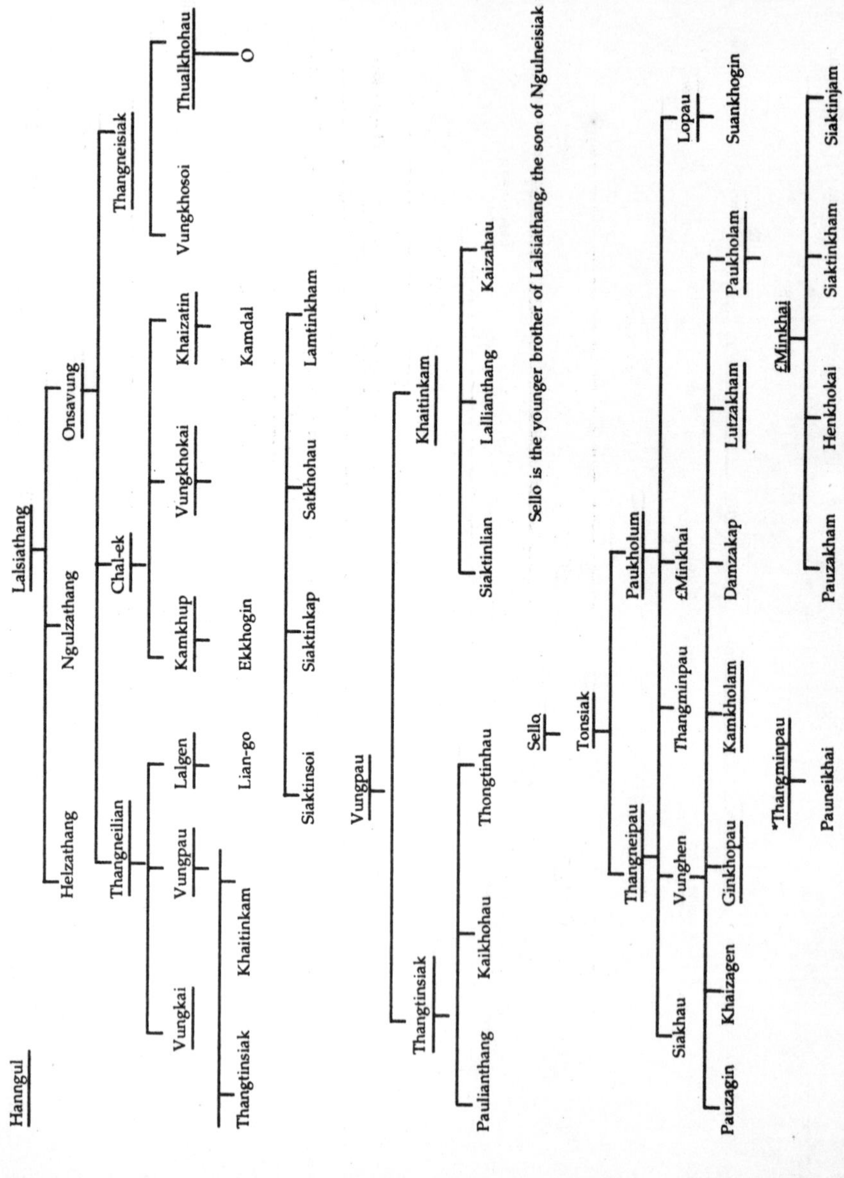

Sello is the younger brother of Lalsiathang, the son of Ngulneisiak

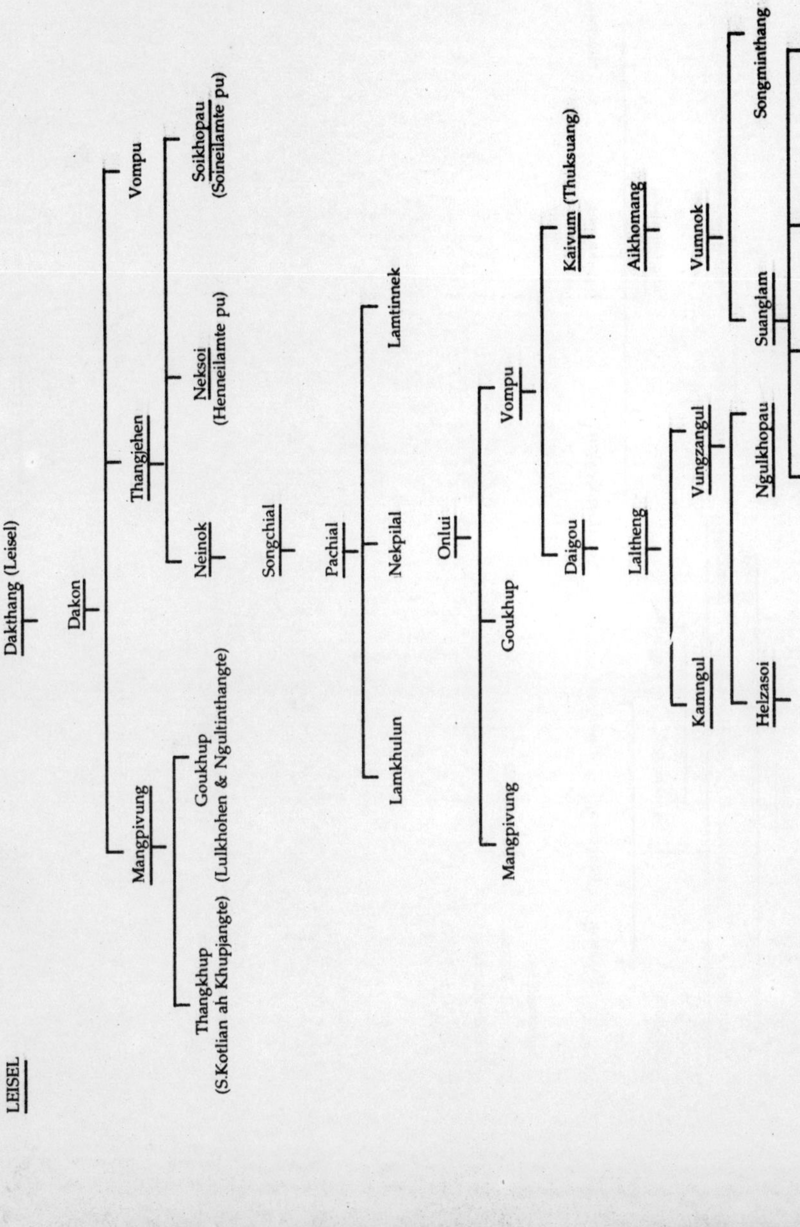
LEISEL
Dakthang (Leisel)
Dakon
Mangpivung
Thangjehen
Vompu
Thangkhup (S.Kotlian ah Khupjangte)
Goukhup (Lulkhohen & Ngultinthangte)
Neinok
Neksoi (Henneilamte pu)
Soikhopau (Soineilamte pu)
Songchial
Pachial
Lamkhulun
Nekpilal
Lamtinnek
Onlui
Mangpivung
Goukhup
Vompu
Daigou
Kaivum (Thuksuang)
Laltheng
Aikhomang
Kamngul
Vungzangul
Vumnok
Helzasoi
Ngulkhopau
Suanglam
Songminthang
Kailam
Vumthang
Mangneilam
Ngulneipau

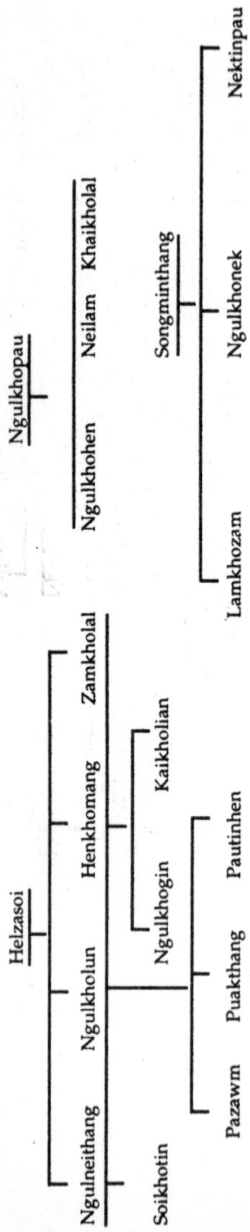

Approved by:
Upa. S. L. Kaicha
Haukhuangching

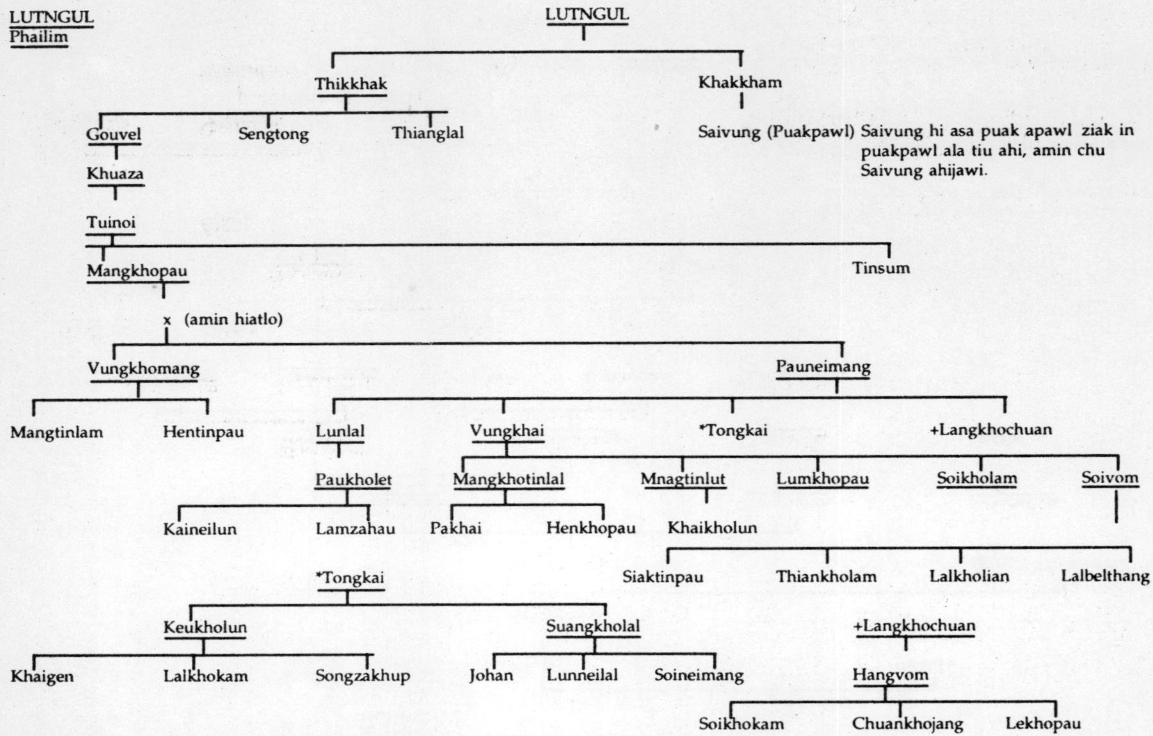

Sengtong is a bastard of Khikkhak, the son of Lutngul, with the daughter of Khuanghau. Though he was not born from the house, he was older than Thianglal. Some Khautes claimed that the father of Sengtong was Tinvuk (the progenitor of the Vangluas) and the mother was a daughter of Suantak families. However the Suantaks say that Chonlu and Sengtong were sons of Lutngul, bastard Chonglu was with the mother's family and Sengtong was with the father's family. Clan and genelogical tree can never be traced from woman's line.

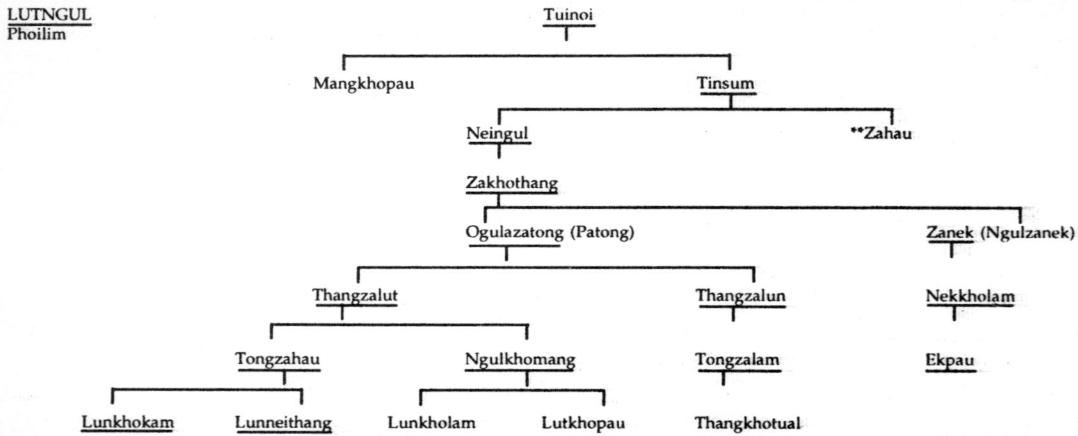

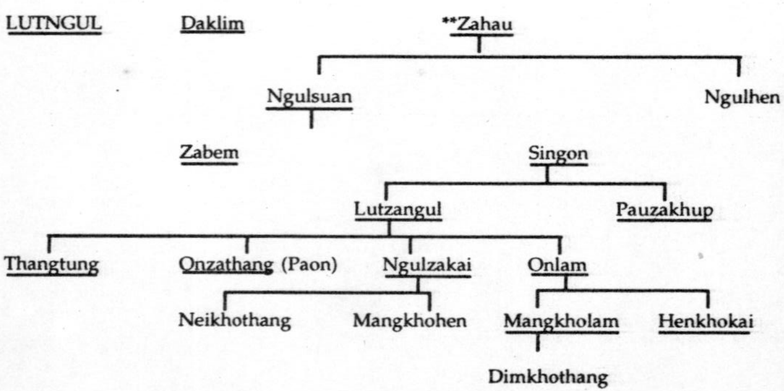

Pu Ngulsuan and pu Ngulhen were rich and had the *chon* feast which was done only by those very rich and high birth.

Pu Zabem was arrested by the enemies when he went to supply rice for his family and he was thrown in the river of Tuivai binding his hands. No one knows his fate.

Pu Pauzakhup was the man who fortified Saram Patong village. He died falling from a tree.

Pu Lutzangul was known as Phaiza galhatpa (hero of Phaiza). Onlam was the son of his second wife Tingkim.

LUTNGUL
Neuzaw sung

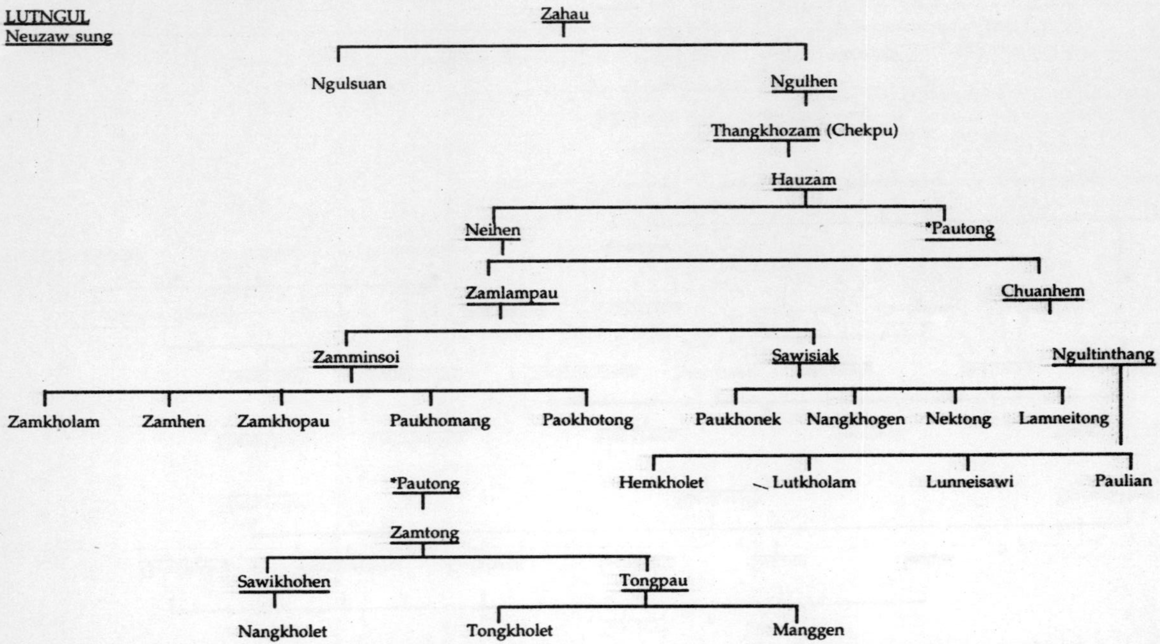

The sons of pu Tuinoi, Tinsum and Mangkhopau were heroes and kings in Chinhills at Phaiza. There is a song praising them as king and hero. The song goes like this "Toimang alal in umhen vabang pau ding Toisum

chawlnga leng bange" and the reply of this goes like this "Toisum thangkawl ni suana, kawtdawng vuisin bang name" (translation `Let Mangkhopau reign for good, for the heroic work there is Tinsum - the fame of Tinsum is known even to the places where the sun rises"

During their reign at phaiza, the Lutngul king said "Sialiap is my village cryer, and Bulte is my priest" (Sialiap ka tangsam, Bulte ka thiampu.

The Lutnguls were famous in the war. They have one Chelthil, which was taken from the people of Phailum/Phaium during their fight. Later on they were defeated and killed. This is the very reason that the number of Lutngul is very small among the Vaipheis.

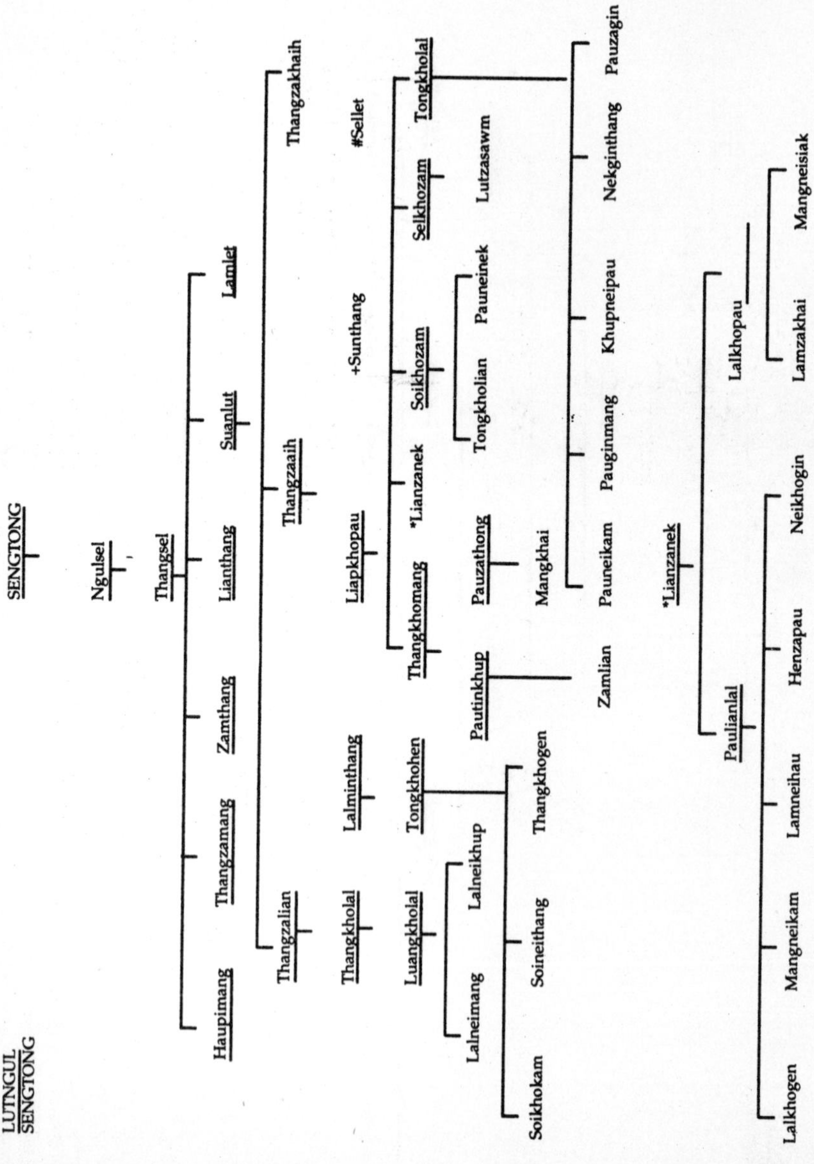
LUTNGUL
SENGTONG
SENGTONG
Ngulsel
Thangsel
Haupimang
Thangzamang
Zamthang
Lianthang
Suanlut
Lamlet
Thangzalian
Thangzaaih
Thangzakhaih
Thangkholal
Lalminthang
Liapkhopau
+Sunthang
#Sellet
Luangkholal
Tongkhohen
Thangkhomang
*Lianzanek
Soikhozam
Selkhozam
Tongkholal
Lalneimang
Lalneikhup
Pautinkhup
Pauzathong
Tongkholian
Pauneinek
Lutzasawm
Soikhokam
Soineithang
Thangkhogen
Mangkhai
Zamlian
Pauneikam
Pauginmang
Khupneipau
Nekginthang
Pauzagin
*Lianzanek
Paulianlal
Lalkhopau
Lalkhogen
Mangneikam
Lamneihau
Henzapau
Neikhogin
Lamzakhai
Mangneisiak

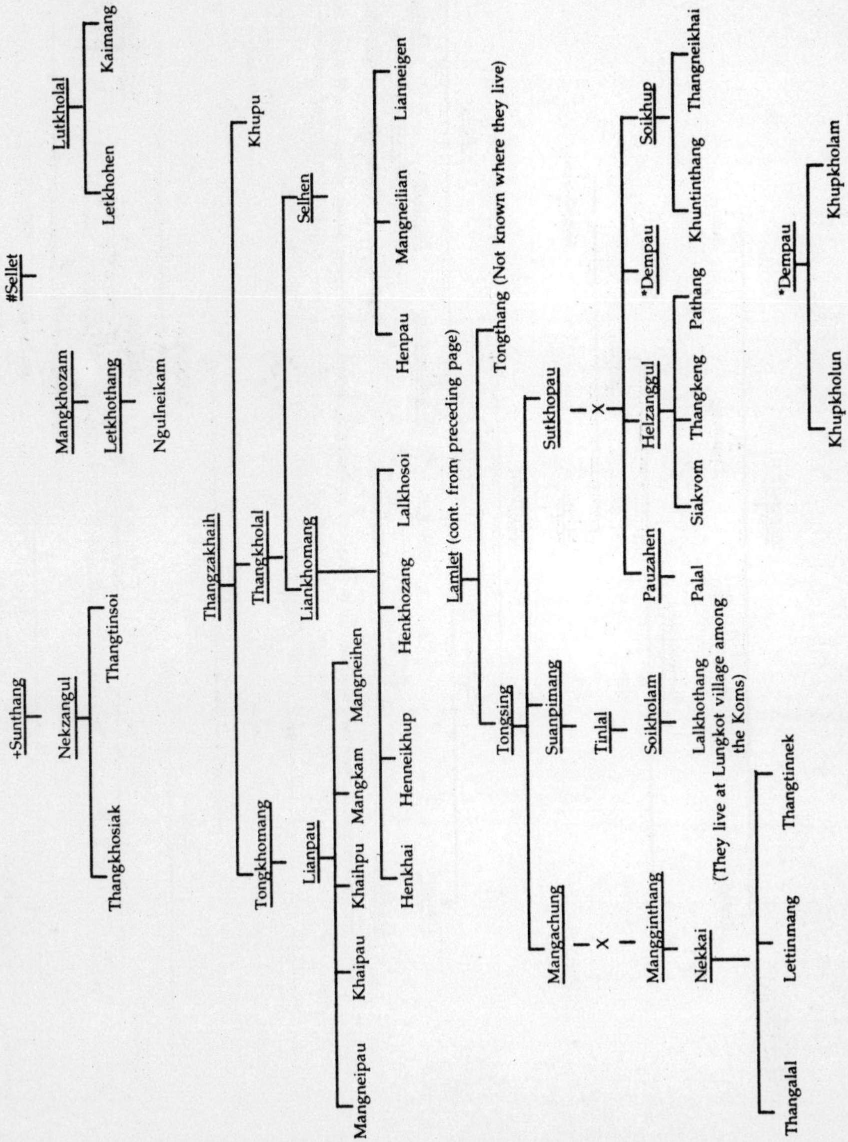

+Sunthang
Nekzangul
Thangkhosiak
Thangtinsoi
Mangkhozam
Letkhothang
Ngulneikam
#Sellet
Lutkholal
Letkhohen
Kaimang
Thangzakhaih
Tongkhomang
Thangkholal
Khupu
Lianpau
Mangneipau
Khaipau
Khaihpu
Mangkam
Mangneihen
Liankhomang
Selhen
Henkhai
Henneikhup
Henkhozang
Lalkhosoi
Henpau
Mangneilian
Lianneigen
Lamlet (cont. from preceding page)
Tongsing
Tongthang (Not known where they live)
Mangachung
Suanpimang
Sutkhopau
X
Manginthang
Tinlal
Soikholam
Pauzahen
Helzanggul
*Dempau
Soikhup
Nekkai
(They live at Lungkot village among the Koms)
Lalkhothang
Palal
Siakvom
Thangkeng
Pathang
Khuntinthang
Thangneikhai
Thangalal
Lettinmang
Thangtinnek
Khupkholun
Khupkholam

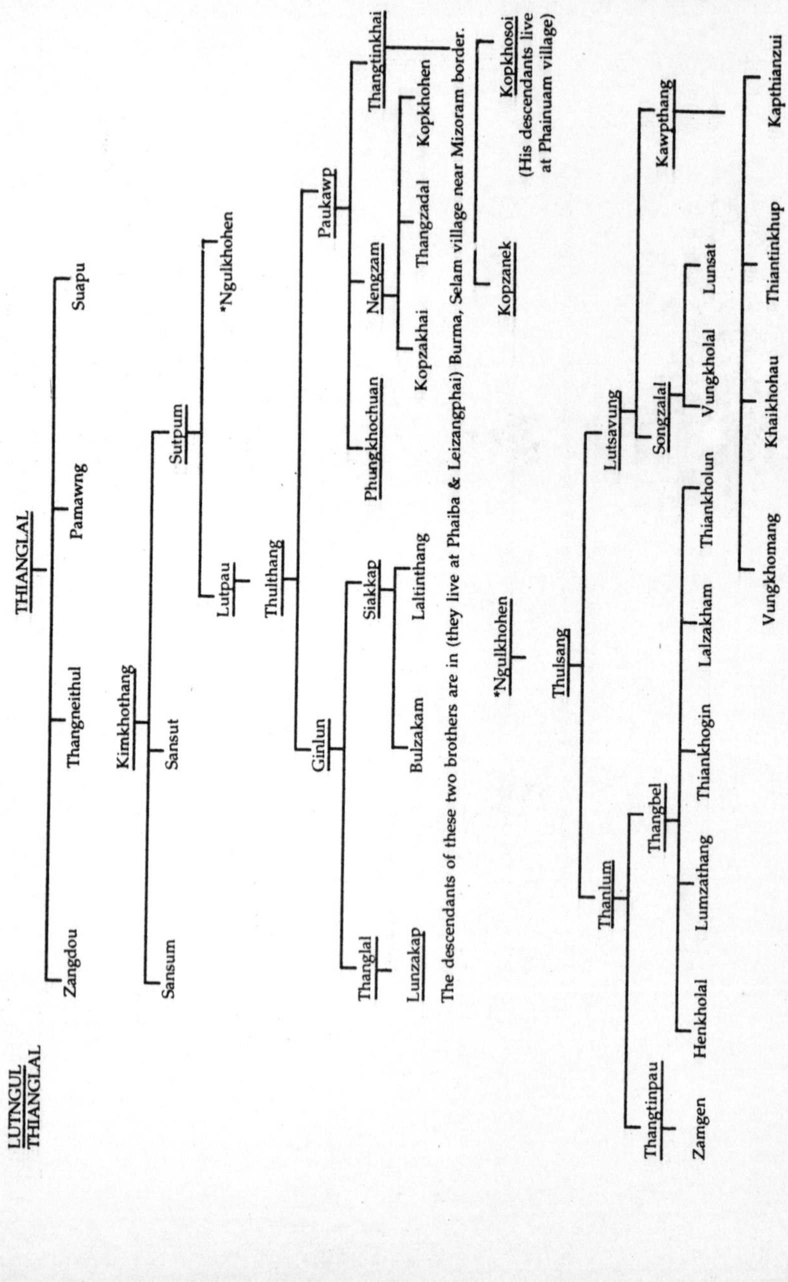
LUTNGUL
THIANGLAL
THIANGLAL
Zangdou
Thangneithul
Pamawng
Suapu
Kimkhothang
Sansum
Sansut
Sutpum
Lutpau
*Ngulkhohen
Thulthang
Ginlun
Paukawp
Thanglal
Lunzakap
Siakkap
Bulzakam
Laltinthang
Phungkhochuan
Nengzam
Thangtinkhai
Kopzakhai
Thangzadal
Kopkhohen
The descendants of these two brothers are in (they live at Phaiba & Leizangphai) Burma, Selam village near Mizoram border.
Kopzanek
Kopkhosoi
(His descendants live at Phainuam village)
*Ngulkhohen
Thulsang
Thanlum
Lutsavung
Thangtinpau
Zamgen
Henkholal
Thangbel
Lumzathang
Thiankhogin
Lalzakham
Thiankholun
Songzalal
Vungkholal
Lunsat
Kawpthang
Vungkhomang
Khaikhohau
Thiantinkhup
Kapthianzui

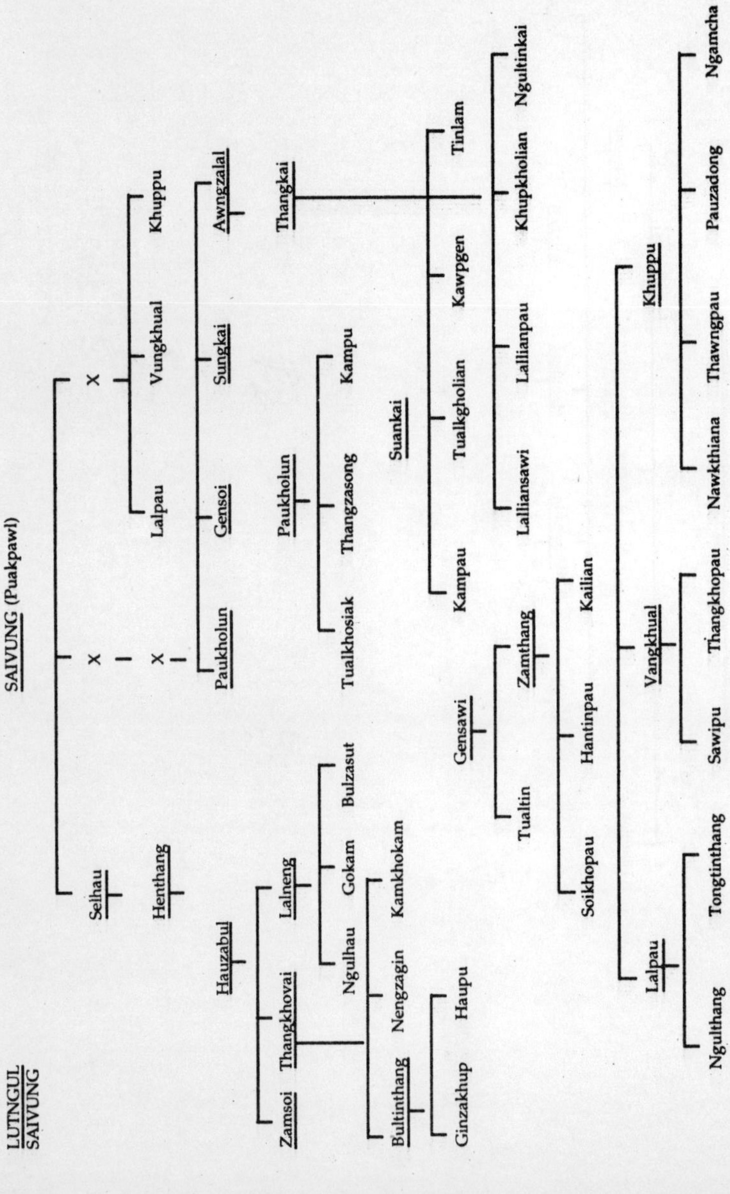

Contributor: Pastor Lalliansawi

Suantak
DORMUL Suantak

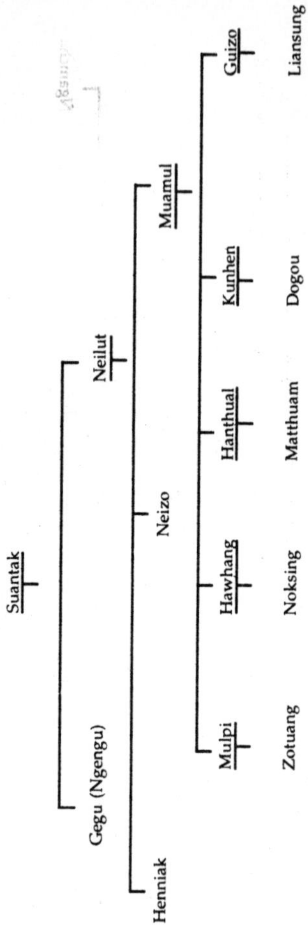

Contributor:
Mr. Lianzakap

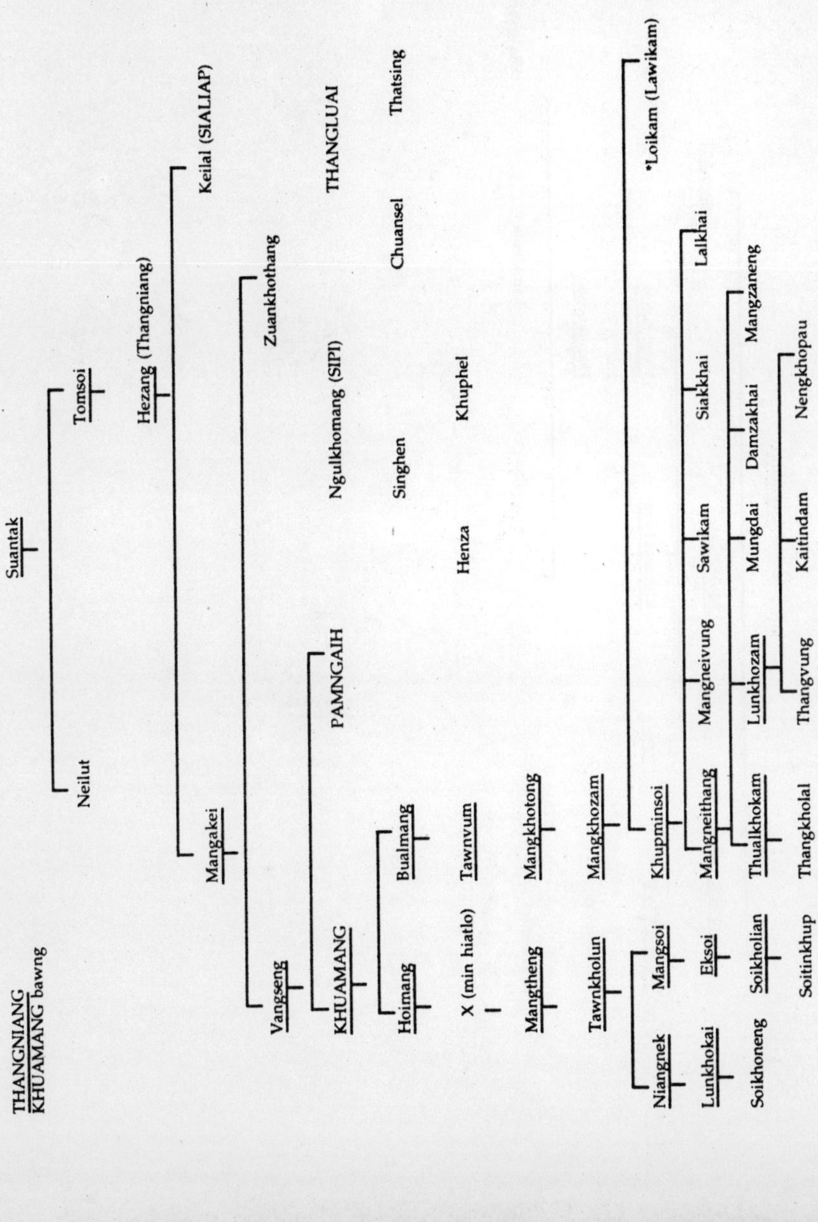
THANGNIANG
KHUAMANG bawng
Suantak
Neilut
Tomsoi
Mangakei
Hezang (Thangniang)
Keilal (SIALIAP)
Vangseng
Zuankhothang
KHUAMANG
PAMNGAIH
Ngulkhomang (SIPI)
THANGLUAI
Hoimang
Bualmang
Singhen
Chuansel
Thatsing
X (min hiatlo)
Tawnvum
Henza
Khuphel
Mangtheng
Mangkhotong
Tawnkholun
Mangkhozam
*Loikam (Lawikam)
Niangnek
Mangsoi
Khupminsoi
Lunkhokai
Eksoi
Mangneithang
Mangneivung
Sawikam
Siakkhai
Lalkhai
Soikhoneng
Soikholian
Thualkhokam
Lunkhozam
Mungdai
Damzakhai
Mangzaneng
Soitinkhup
Thangkholal
Thangvung
Kaitindam
Nengkhopau

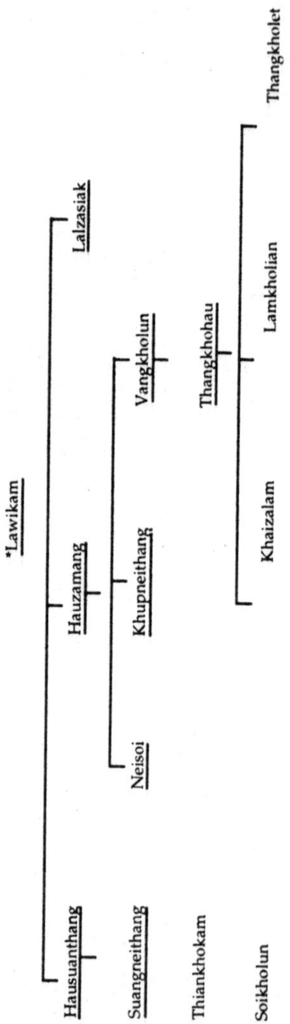
*Lawikam
Hausuanthang
Hauzamang
Lalzasiak
Suangneithang
Neisoi
Khupneithang
Vangkholun
Thiankhokam
Thangkhohau
Soikholun
Khaizalam
Lamkholian
Thangkholet

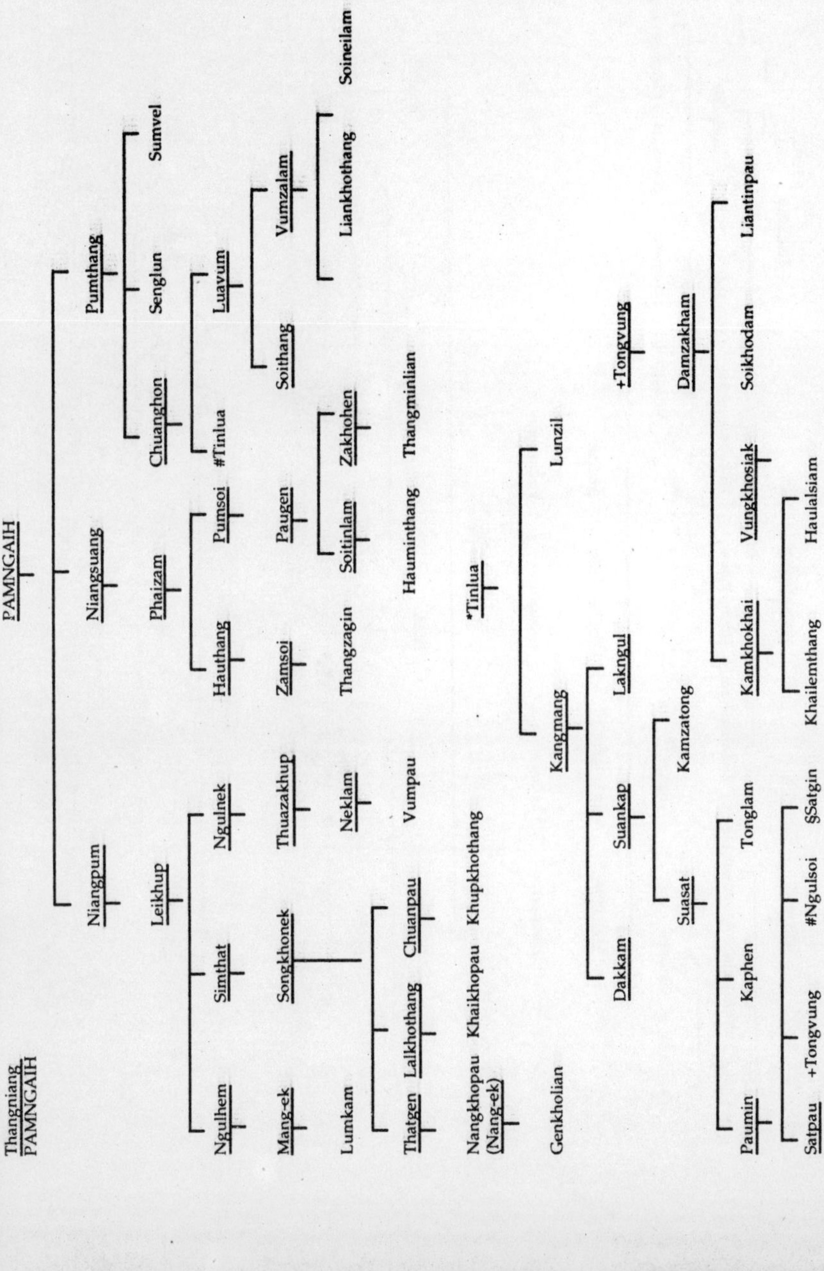
Thangniang
PAMNGAIH
PAMNGAIH
Niangpum
Niangsuang
Pumthang
Leikhup
Phaizam
Chuanghon
Senglun
Sumvel
Ngulhem
Simthat
Ngulnek
Hauthang
Pumsoi
#Tinlua
Luavum
Mang-ek
Songkhonek
Thuazakhup
Zamsoi
Paugen
Soithang
Vumzalam
Lumkam
Neklam
Thangzagin
Soitinlam
Zakhohen
Liankhothang
Soineilam
Thatgen
Lalkhothang
Chuanpau
Vumpau
Hauminthang
Thangminlian
Nangkhopau
(Nang-ek)
Khaikhopau
Khupkhothang
*Tinlua
Genkholian
Kangmang
Lunzil
Dakkam
Suankap
Lakngul
+Tongvung
Suasat
Kamzatong
Damzakham
Paumin
Kaphen
Tonglam
Kamkhokhai
Vungkhosiak
Soikhodam
Liantinpau
Satpau
+Tongvung
#Ngulsoi
§Satgin
Khailemthang
Haulalsiam

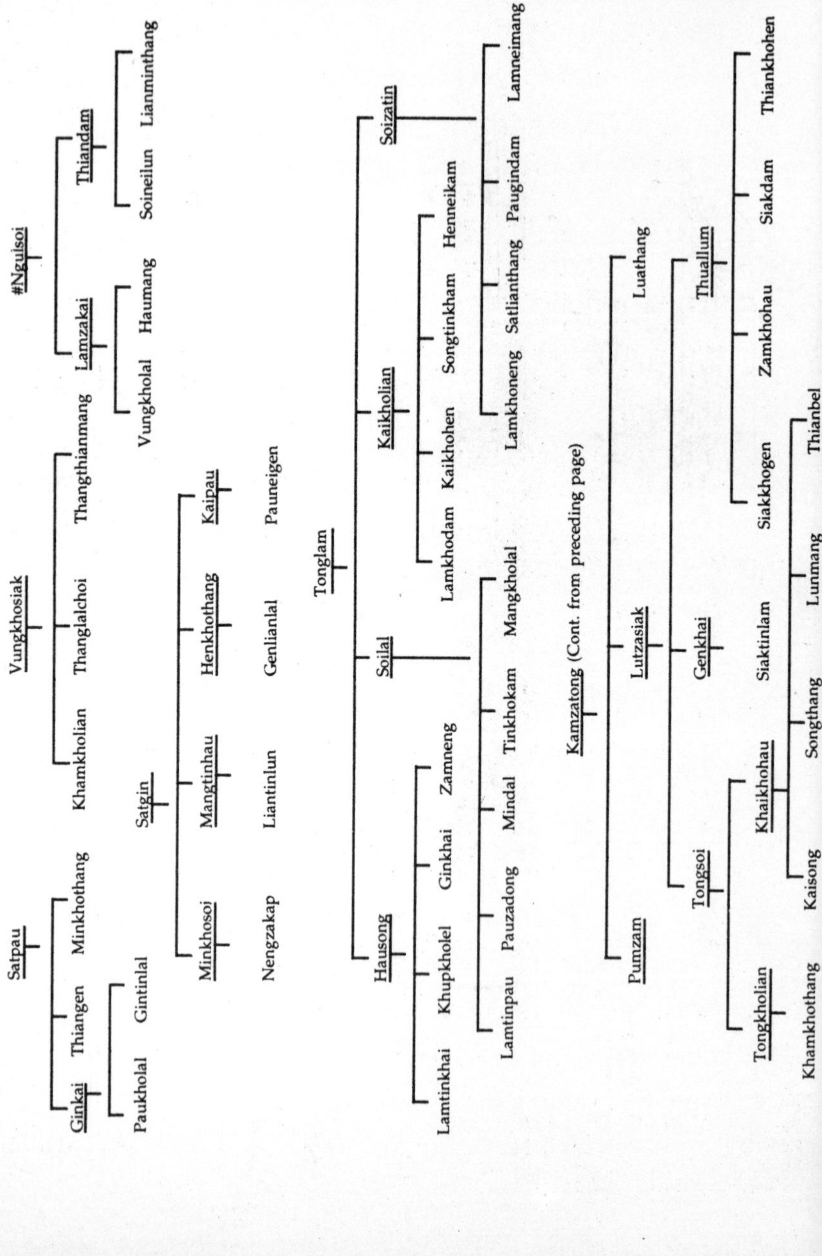

Satpau
Ginkai
Thiangen
Minkhothang
Paukholal
Gintinlal
Vungkhosiak
Khamkholian
Thanglalchoi
Thangthianmang
#Ngulsoi
Lamzakai
Thiandam
Vungkholal
Haumang
Soineilun
Lianminthang
Satgin
Minkhosoi
Mangtinhau
Henkhothang
Kaipau
Nengzakap
Liantinlun
Genlianlal
Pauneigen
Tonglam
Hausong
Soilal
Kaikholian
Soizatin
Lamtinkhai
Khupkholel
Ginkhai
Zamneng
Lamkhodam
Kaikhohen
Songtinkham
Henneikam
Lamtinpau
Pauzadong
Mindal
Tinkhokam
Mangkholal
Lamkhoneng
Satlianthang
Paugindam
Lamneimang
Kamzatong (Cont. from preceding page)
Pumzam
Lutzasiak
Luathang
Tongsoi
Genkhai
Thuallum
Tongkholian
Khaikhohau
Khamkhothang
Kaisong
Songthang
Lunmang
Thianbel
Siaktinlam
Siakkhogen
Zamkhohau
Siakdam
Thiankhohen

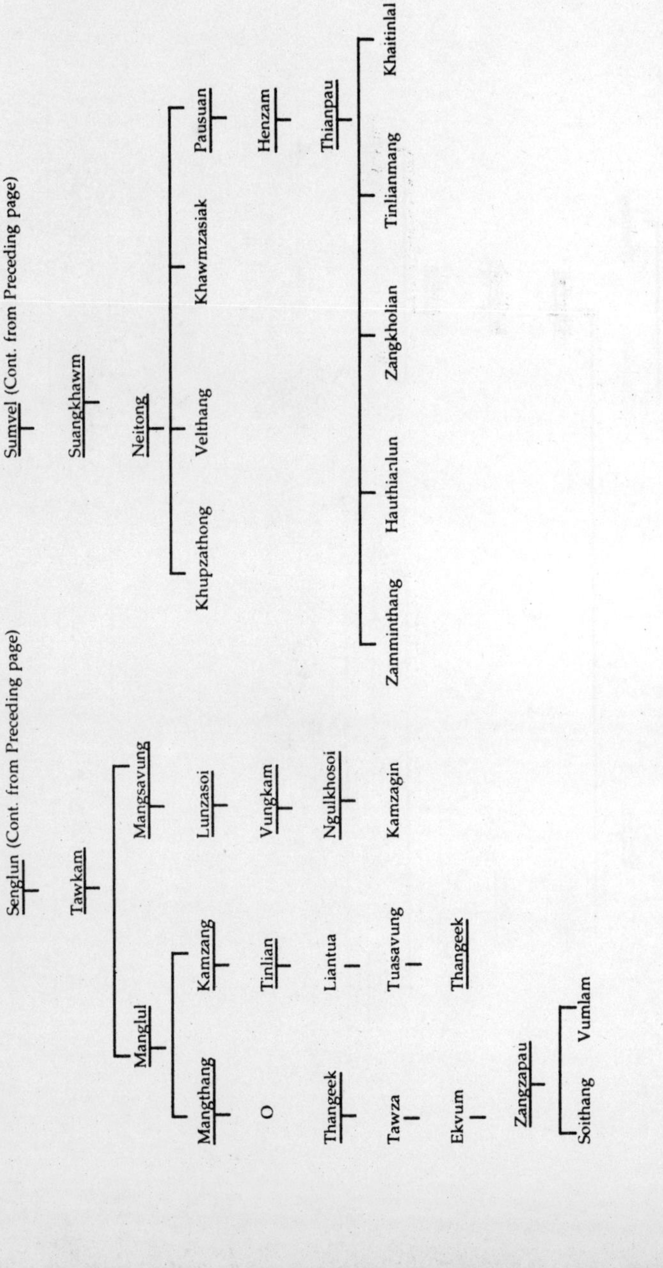
Senglun (Cont. from Preceding page)
Tawkam
Manglul
Mangsavung
Mangthang
Kamzang
Lunzasoi
O
Tinlian
Vungkam
Thangeek
Liantua
Ngulkhosoi
Tawza
Tuasavung
Kamzagin
Ekvum
Thangeek
Zangzapau
Soithang
Vumlam
Sumvel (Cont. from Preceding page)
Suangkhawm
Neitong
Khupzathong
Velthang
Khawmzasiak
Pausuan
Henzam
Thianpau
Zamminthang
Hauthianlun
Zangkholian
Tinlianmang
Khaitinlal

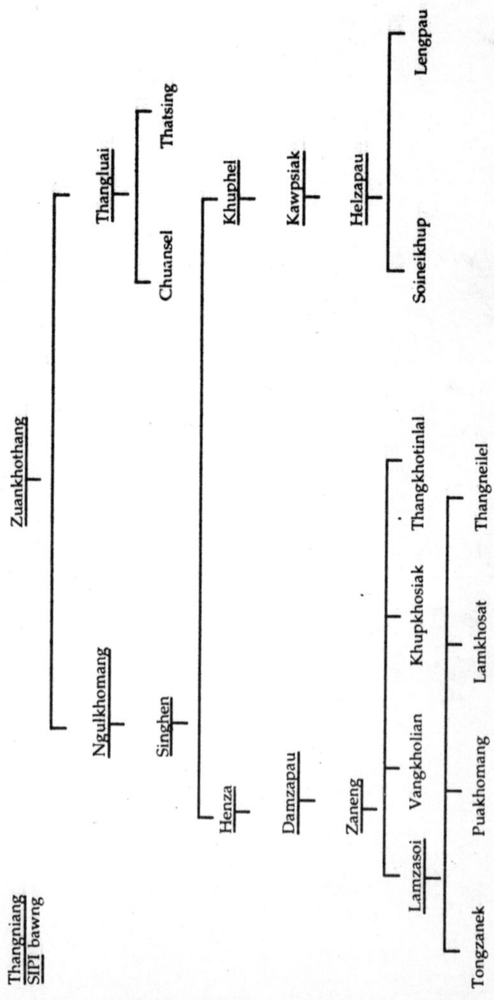
Thangniang
SIPI bawng
Zuankhothang
Ngulkhomang
Thangluai
Singhen
Chuansel
Thatsing
Henza
Khuphel
Damzapau
Kawpsiak
Zaneng
Helzapau
Lamzasoi
Vangkholian
Khupkhosiak
Thangkhotinlal
Soineikhup
Lengpau
Tongzanek
Puakhomang
Lamkhosat
Thangneilel

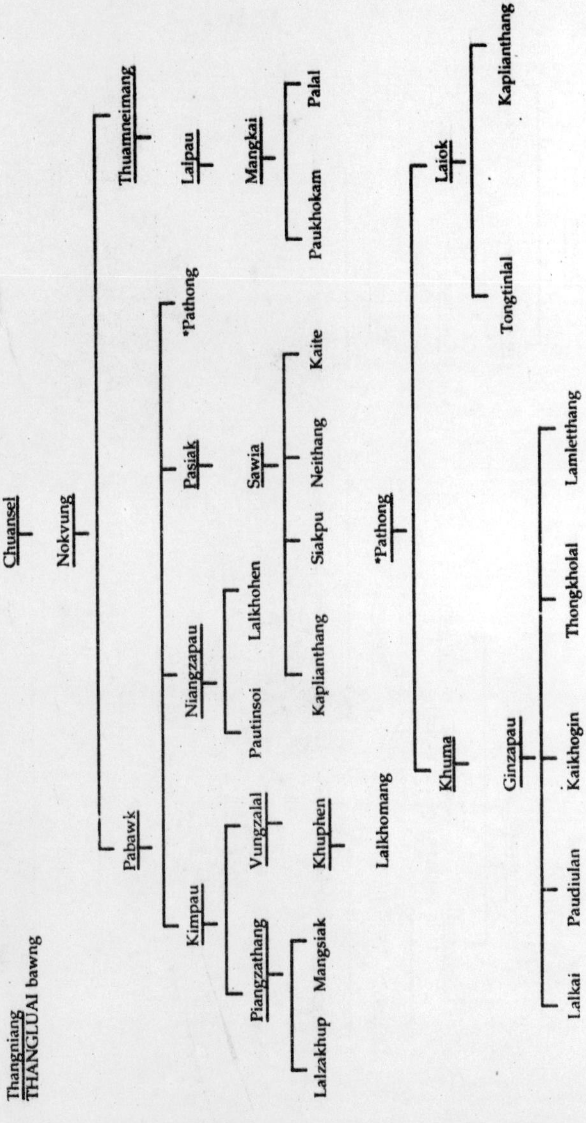

Thangniang
THANGLUAI bawng
Chuansel
Nokvung
Pabawk
Thuamneimang
Kimpau
Niangzapau
Pasiak
*Pathong
Lalpau
Piangzathang
Vungzalal
Pautinsoi
Lalkhohen
Sawia
Mangkai
Lalzakhup
Mangsiak
Khuphen
Kaplianthang
Siakpu
Neithang
Kaite
Paukhokam
Palal
Lalkhomang
*Pathong
Khuma
Laiok
Tongtinlal
Kaplianthang
Ginzapau
Lalkai
Paudiulan
Kaikhogin
Thongkholal
Lamletthang

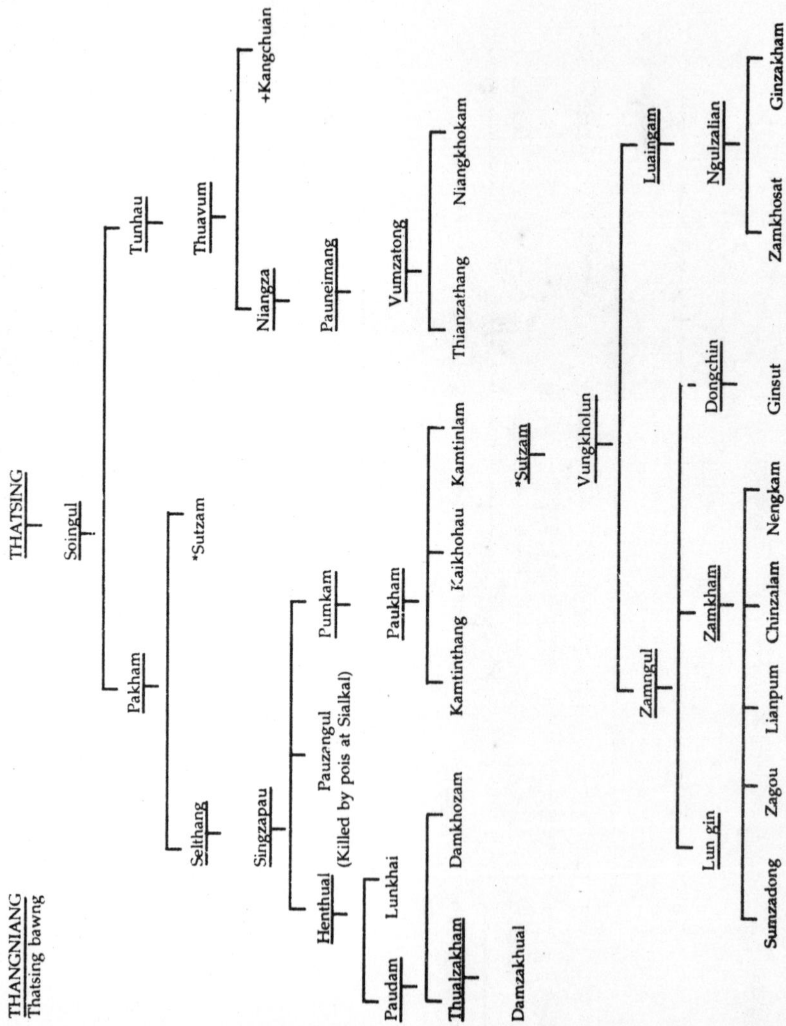
THANGNIANG
Thatsing bawng
THATSING
Soingul
Pakham
Tunhau
Selthang
*Sutzam
Thuavum
Niangza
+Kangchuan
Singzapau
Henthual
Pauzangul
(Killed by pois at Sialkal)
Pumkam
Pauneimang
Paudam
Lunkhai
Paukham
Vumzatong
Thualzakham
Damkhozam
Kamtinthang
Kaikhohau
Kamtinlam
Thianzathang
Niangkhokam
Damzakhual
*Sutzam
Vungkholun
Zamngul
Luaingam
Lun gin
Zamkham
Dongchin
Ngulzalian
Sumzadong
Zagou
Lianpum
Chinzalam
Nengkam
Ginsut
Zamkhosat
Ginzakham

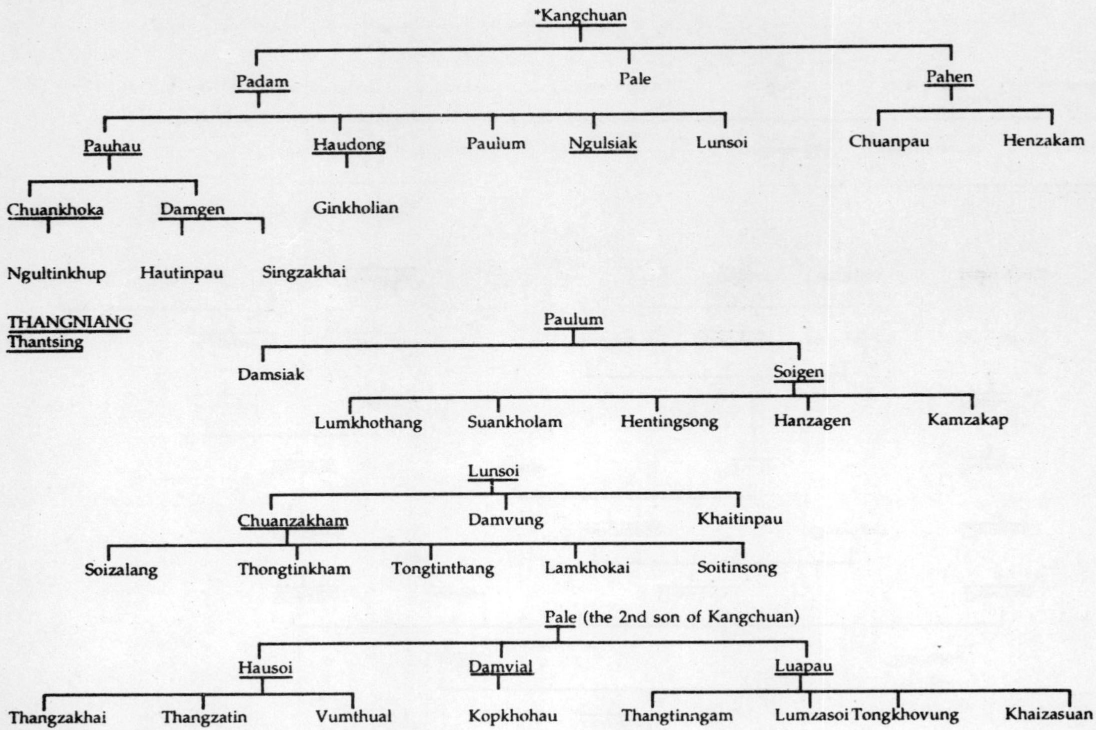

Contributors:-

1. Mr. L. Thanglet, Churachandpur
2. Dr. Damzakhai, Imphal
3. Mr. Lamtinkhai, Imphal
4. Mr. Paukholal,Pengzang

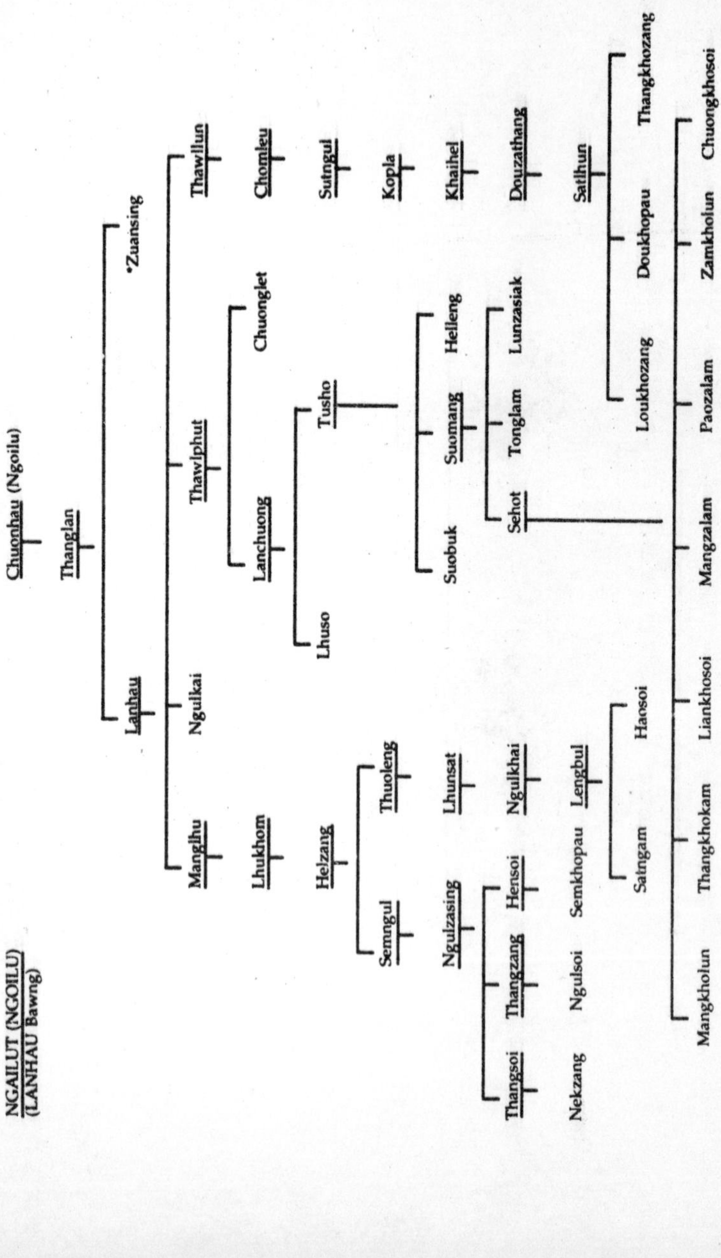
NGAILUT (NGOILU)
(LANHAU Bawng)
Chuonhau (Ngoilu)
Thanglan
Lanhau
*Zuansing
Manglhu
Ngulkai
Thawlphut
Thawllun
Lhukhom
Lanchuong
Chuonglet
Chomleu
Helzang
Lhuso
Tusho
Sutngul
Semngul
Thuoleng
Kopla
Ngulzasing
Lhunsat
Suobuk
Suomang
Helleng
Khaihel
Thangsoi
Thangzang
Hensoi
Ngulkhai
Sehot
Tonglam
Lunzasiak
Douzathang
Nekzang
Ngulsoi
Semkhopau
Lengbul
Satlhun
Satngam
Haosoi
Loukhozang
Doukhopau
Thangkhozang
Mangkholun
Thangkhokam
Liankhosoi
Mangzalam
Paozalam
Zamkholun
Chuongkhosoi

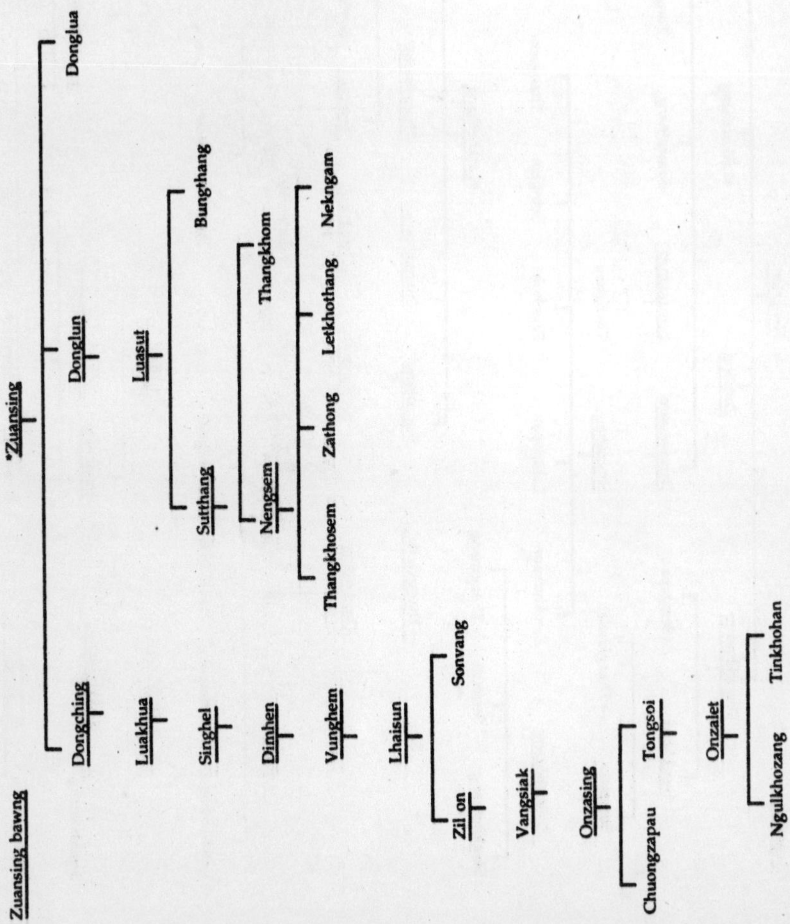
Zuansing bawng
*Zuansing
Dongching
Donglun
Donglua
Luakhua
Luasut
Singhel
Sutthang
Bungthang
Dimhen
Nengsem
Thangkhom
Vunghen
Thangkhosem
Zathong
Letkhothang
Nekngam
Lhaisun
Zil on
Sonvang
Vangsiak
Onzasing
Chuongzapau
Tongsoi
Onzalet
Ngulkhozang
Tinkhohan

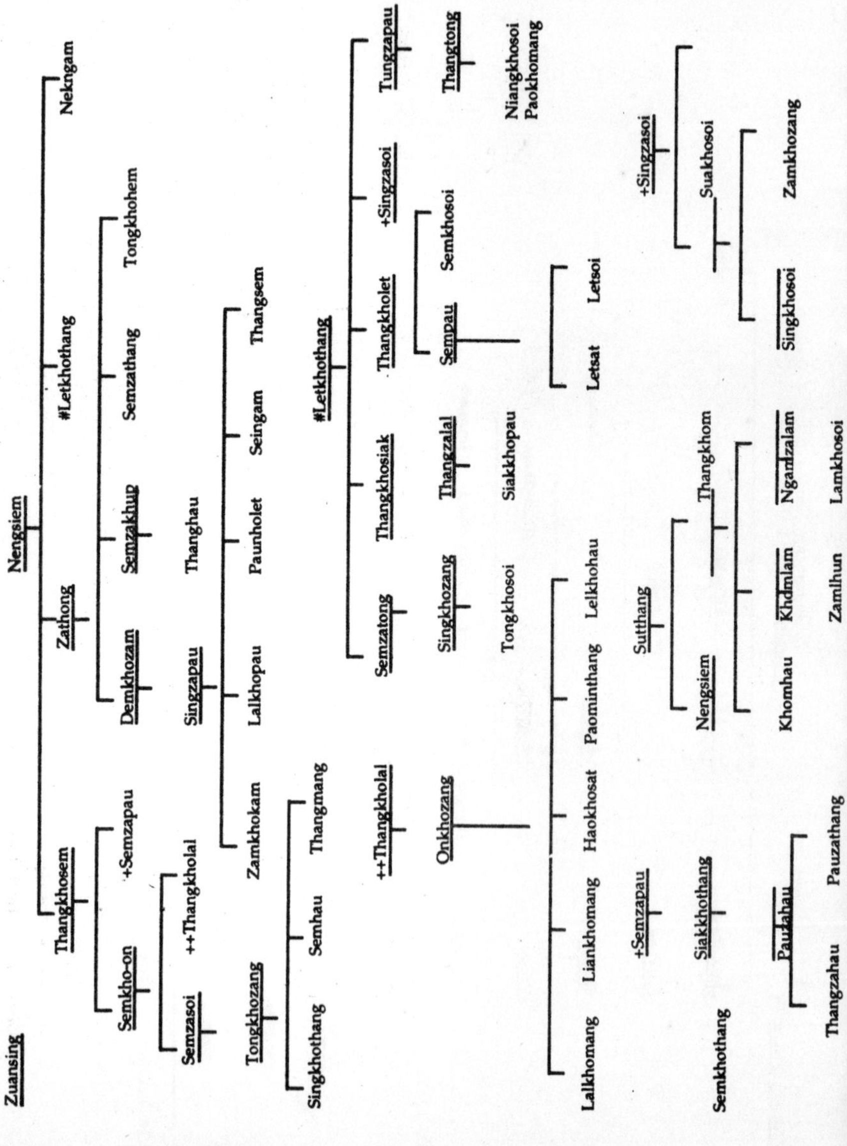
Zuansing
Nengsiem
Thangkhosem
Zathong
#Letkhothang
Nekngam
Semkho-on
+Semzapau
Demkhozam
Semzakhup
Semzathang
Tongkhohem
Semzasoi
++Thangkholal
Singzapau
Thanghau
Zamkhokam
Lalkhopau
Paunholet
Seingam
Thangsem
Tongkhozang
Singkhothang
Semhau
Thangmang
++Thangkholal
Semzatong
Thangkhosiak
#Letkhothang
Thangkholet
+Singzasoi
Tungzapau
Onkhozang
Singkhozang
Thangzalal
Sempau
Semkhosoi
Thangtong
Tongkhosoi
Siakkhopau
Niangkhosoi
Paokhomang
Lalkhomang
Liankhomang
Haokhosat
Paominthang
Lelkhohau
Letsat
Letsoi
+Semzapau
Sutthang
+Singzasoi
Semkhothang
Siakkhothang
Nengsiem
Thangkhom
Suakhosoi
Pauzahau
Khomhau
Khomlam
Ngamzalam
Singkhosoi
Zamkhozang
Thangzahau
Pauzathang
Zamlhun
Lamkhosoi

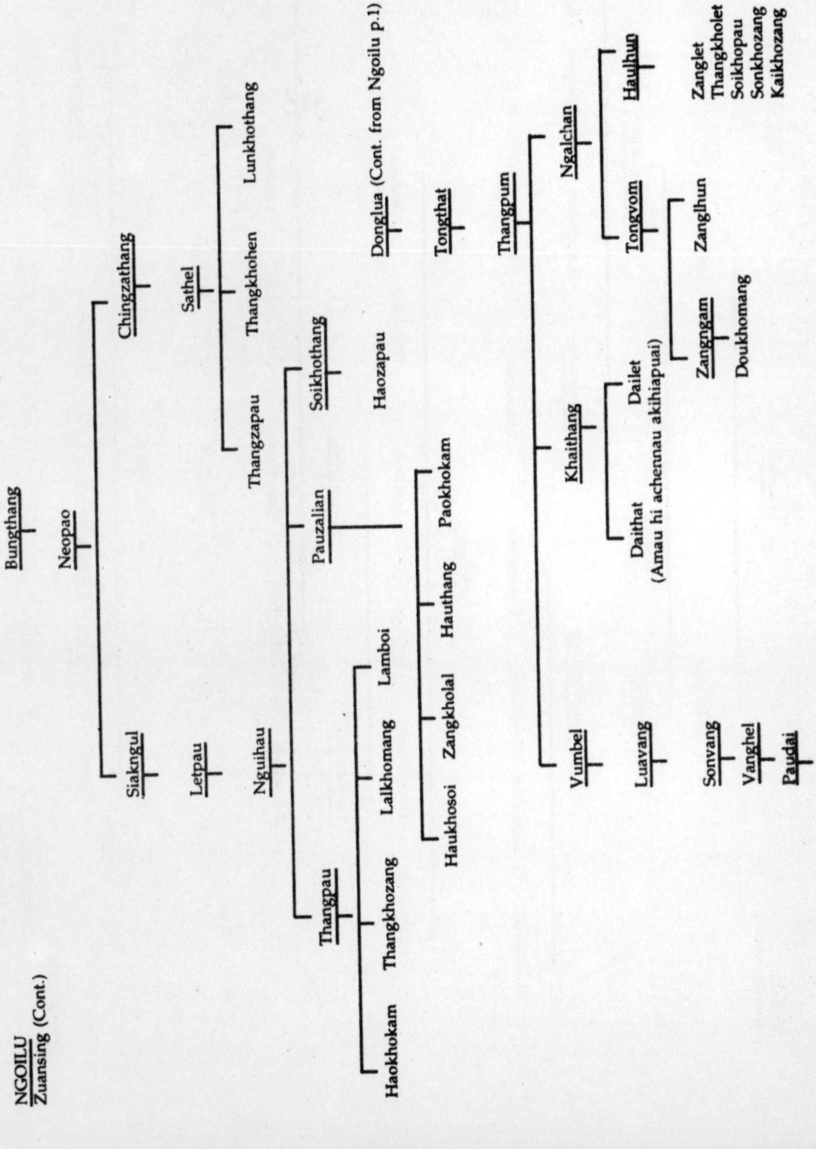
NGOILU
Zuansing (Cont.)
Bungthang
Neopao
Siakngul
Chingzathang
Letpau
Sathel
Thangzapau
Thangkhohen
Lunkhothang
Nguihau
Thangpau
Pauzalian
Soikhothang
Haokhokam
Thangkhozang
Lalkhomang
Lamboi
Haozapau
Donglua (Cont. from Ngoilu p.1)
Haukhosoi
Zangkholal
Hauthang
Paokhokam
Tongthat
Thangpum
Vumbel
Khaithang
Ngalchan
Luavang
Daithat
(Amau hi achennau akihiapuai)
Dailet
Tongvom
Haulhun
Sonvang
Zangngam
Zanglhun
Vanghel
Doukhomang
Paudai
Zanglet
Thangkholet
Soikhopau
Sonkhozang
Kaikhozang

NEOILU
Zuansing (cont.)

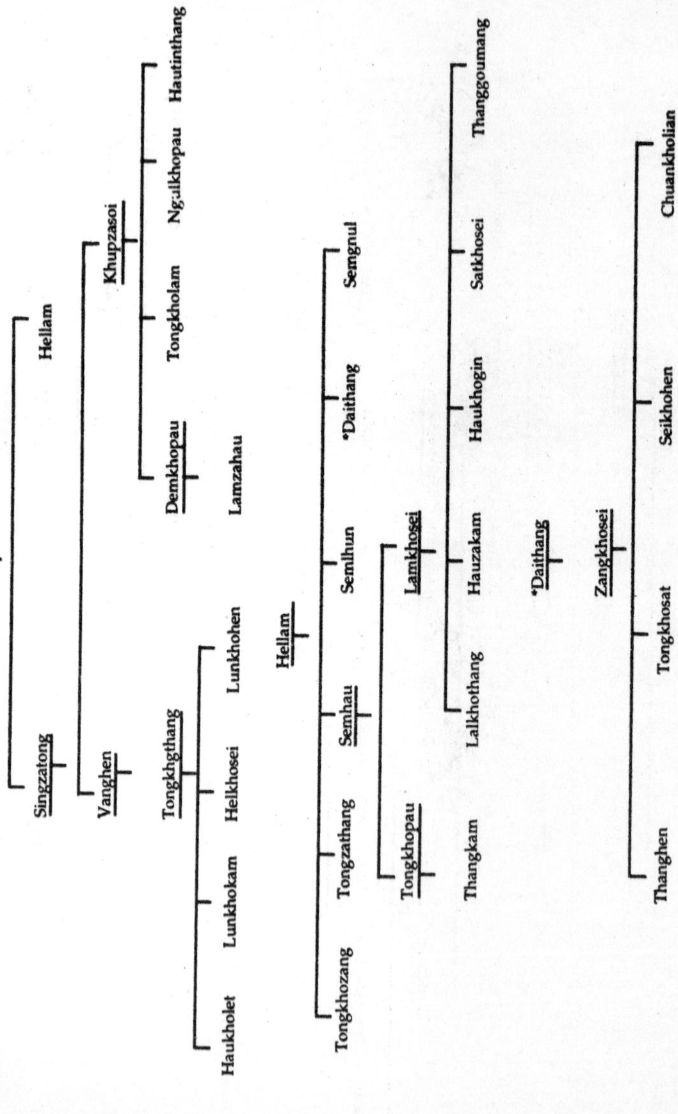

Contributors:

1. Demkhopau
2. Pastor Tongkholam
3. Helkhosei

CHULZANG

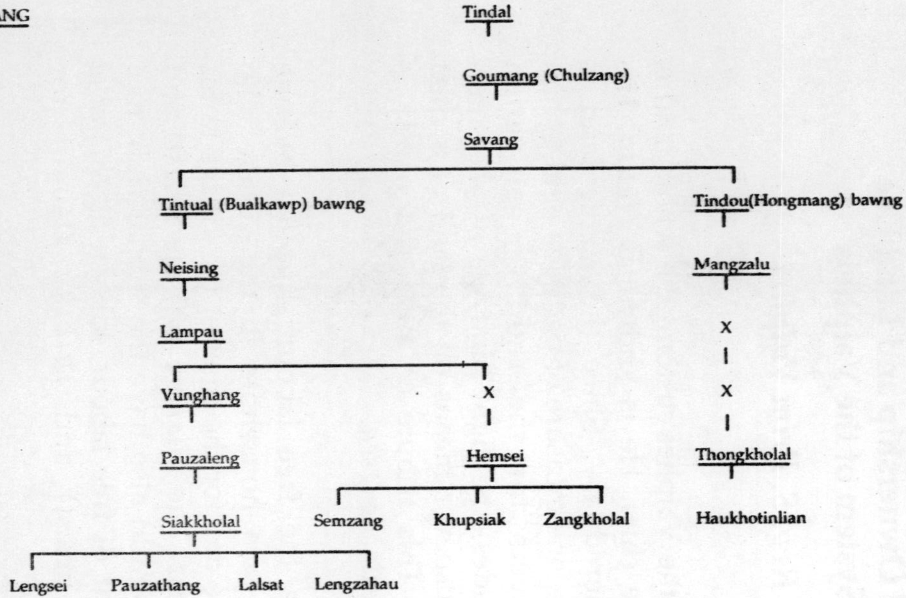

It is said that Goumang had two sons, the older one is Sevang and the younger one is Keivom.

Thongkholal's ancestors lived 3/4 generations among the Songlhou (Sekzang). When pu Lampau went to redeem them and tried to give Rs.40/- as ransom, the housemother of Sekzang said 'You don't need to pay me ransom, they are not my slave". Hearing this pu Lampau came back.

It is very difficult to get information about the geneological tree of the Chulzang. If someone knows better than this, let's correct next time.

CHAPTER IX

Land Ownership and Land Use System of the Vaipheis

Rev. S. Prim Vaiphei

According to the Vaiphei custom, the whole land is owned by the chief. He is known as *Hausa*. His position is hereditary. Since the whole land is owned by him, one measure of paddy is paid to him by the villagers for the right of cultivation annually. Besides, the right hind leg of all games killed by whatsoever means on the land of a chief goes to him. This tribute of meat and paddy is known as *samal changseu.*

Khuatha is the free labour supplied by one person from each household in the village who must work one day for the chief of the village in his field every year. The *thiampu* (village priest) and *thiksek* (blacksmith) also have the similar right to a certain amount of free labour, known as *thiamtha* (labour for priest) and *thiktha* (labour for blacksmith).

Every year, the village authority decided on the area where they should cultivate their jhuming cultivation. They then distribute the area, say one acre each to each family. After this, every family cut their portion of the land for their own cultivation. The authority assigned land according to the size of the family. No one is allowed to choose the area for his own cultivation. Thus after ten years or more, the same area shall be cultivated again. They don't cultivate a plot more than one year. If a person wants to terrace one area for wet cultivation, he should obtain permission from the village chief. Such kind of terraced cultivation is not common among the Vaipheis.

If someone from other village wanted to have jhuming cultivation within the land of a chief, he should approach the chief and the chief can reject or grant the request at his own will. If he is allowed to cultivate, he should give a share to the chief as tax for the land.

The chief being the owner of the whole land has every right to drive out the families whom he does not like, from his village. Even if he does not drive them out, he has the right not to assign land for cultivation to those families. If a family migrates to another village, all the immovable properties within the land should go to the chief, e.g. if he has a mango tree, orange tree or kitchen garden, these should go to the chief after he left the village. Even the house building should go to the chief.

The chief also has the right to sell the whole land to other people. If a village is purchased from a certain chief, the villagers shall become the subjects of the new chief who purchased the village. Because of these powers of the chief, the chief of a Kuki-Chin village is known as *Ningthou* and the chief of a Naga village is known as *Khullakpa*.

Village Council

The head of the village is the chief, under him are *Semang, Pachong, Tunpu* and *Changluai*. They are selected by the village council with the consent of the chief. In some cases the chief appoints them by his own authority.

Semang is in charge of the village administration under the chief. He has the right to judge any case and without him no case can be discussed. The meaning of *Semang* is something like honoured. The chief has the right to dethrone him at anytime if he finds some mischief in his work.

Pachong. The word *Pachong* means mighty. It comes from the word *Chong* which means might or brave. His main work is to collect the tributes and tax. All the cases come to *Semang* through

Changluai who is the runner similar to a *choukidar*.

Tunpu is the head of the youth and also a song leader. The name *Tunpu* itself means the man in whose house many people take rest. His house is something like the head office of the village youth society. However, the *Tunpu* is not common today anymore.

If a person sets up a village, his *bechapa* (which will be discussed in detail later) shall be the *Semang* and his younger brothers shall be the *Pachong*.

Tangsam is the man responsible for passing information in the village. He shouts and informs the villagers all the informations they need to know. He informs the villagers the instructions given to him by the *Semang* and *Pachong*.

Every dispute between persons must be brought to the chief through the *Semang* and *Pachong* with a jar of *zu* (rice beer). Leaders of each family gather together in the house of the chief to try the case. The guilty one is fined by one jar of *zu*, one pig and one *muthun* according to the seriousness of the case. This is known as *Salam sat*. The village council is formed by representatives from each clan.

Sapang is a kind of share to the village elders. If a person kills a quadruped, either wild or domestic animal, the village elders must have a share in it called *sapang*. The village elders who eat this *sapang* have great responsibility, like the village guardians. If there is a plague or epidemic that makes all the villagers to run away from the village because of fear, these elders are responsible to bury the dead. If a baby dies right after birth, these elders should bury the dead child without informing the public. If a person is seriously sick from a communicable disease or epidemic, they must look after him.

Chieftainship

If a person dies having a male child, his wife can stay in the house with her children. If she has no male child, she will have to go back to her father and her female children shall go to the brothers of their deceased father. However if the widow likes to live with her children, she can do so, but she has no right to sell the properties of her deceased husband, and the daughters also do not have any claim in the properties.

If a chief with a male child dies, his wife shall look after her children and if he has younger brothers, the younger brother next to him shall look after the village administration until the son of the deceased chief grows up. If the chief has no brother at all, his widow can look after the village administration with the help of *Semang* and *Pachong*.

If a person, after marriage and having children dies and has unmarried younger brothers, the younger brother next to him should marry the widow of his deceased brother and should look after the children of his brother as his own. But now, it is no more compulsory, it has become voluntary. As we shall discuss later, no woman has any right to inherit the properties of her father. The parents should be with their eldest son. It is the responsibility of the eldest son to look after the parents. The properties of the parents should also belong to him. He shall distribute the properties of his father to his younger brothers at his will. The father should advise his eldest son to share the properties with the younger ones. In many cases, the father distributes the properties to his children before he dies.

The parents, when they become old are not allowed to live in the house of their daughters. It will be insulting to the son if his parents choose to live with their daughters. Even if the parents are in the house of their daughters due to some exceptional reasons, they are not expected to die in the house of their daughter.

Incident: In the early 1980s, Mrs. Neikhonem's mother lived with her and died in her house. Mrs. Neikhonem buried her at Chingmeirong Christian Cemetery. The funeral service was conducted under the auspicious of Lamphel Baptist Church. However when the younger brother of Mrs.

Neikhonem heard this, he hired one jeep and came to Imphal. He digged out the corpse from the cemetery and carried it home and buried it in his village.

Law of Inheritance and Women

The Vaipheis, like the other Kuki-Chin tribes, are both patriarchal and patrilineal. No female has any right to inherit the properties of her father nor any genealogical tree can ever be traced on to female line. If a Vaiphei father has no male issue of his own, his properties including the right to claim bride price and even his debts go to his elder brother or the son of his elder brother. If he has no elder brother or brother, it goes to the nearest male relative or next of kin. For better understanding let us see the following chart.

Thongkhohau

Thangkhup Thangpau Neikim (f) Thanghen Hoinu (f)

Haulian Tongkam Hauthang Thanglet

Haupu Kimbem (f) Letpu

Paukhup Veinu(f)

Thongkhohau has three sons, Thangkhup, Thangpau and Thanghen and two daughters, Neikim and Hoinu. The youngest daughter having married has a son called Thanglet. When Thanglet dies, then his son (Letpu) is his heir. The bride price of Hoinu goes to Thongkhohau if alive. If Thongkhohau is already dead, his eldest son Thangkhup is the heir. When Veinu the granddaughter of Thangpau got married, the first *mithun* of her price which is known as *man mala* goes to *Haupu*.

Luangman: Though inheritance and genealogical tree do not follow female line, the seed of women are not neglected. When Thanglet the son of Hoinu, and Tongkam the son of Neikim die, their children will have to give one *mithun* each to *Haupu*. This is known as *Luangman* (meaning the cost of the corpse). If Tongkam the son of Neikim dies having debts it should be paid by their male relatives or next of kin and never by the male descendants of Thognkhohau. If Haupu dies without having a son, all his properties will be inherited by Haulian. Kimbem, his own sister does not have the right to inherit. If he has any debt too it will be paid by Haulian not by Kimbem.

Naming: The sons of a father should name their sons after the name of their father. If we see the chart, Thangkhup, Thangpau, Thanghen named their sons after the name of their father Thongkhohau. Thongkhohau-Haupu; Thongkhohau-Haulian; Thongkhohau-Hauthang. So also their daughters should be named after their grandmother. When the second son is born, he can be named after the name of his mother's father. My first son is named after my father and my second son is named after my wife's father. My father has the freedom to choose either the name of my wife's father or his own name for naming my second son.

Sating is the flesh between the upper sides of the ribs of animals killed by whatsoever means. It is given to the eldest male next of kin. The male descendents of Thangpau and Thanghen should give 'sating' to the eldest male line of Haupu.

Sangong means the neck of animal. When an animal is killed, the neck of the same should be given to the next of kin of his mother. Now if we see again the chart, if Kimbem's son kills an animal, he should give the neck to Haupu. So also if Veinu's sons kill an animal, the neck should be given to Paukhup.

Becha: This word, though very important among the Vaipheis, cannot be translated into English. Each Vaiphei family appoints two or more families in the village to be *bechas*, one of them as the head *Becha* known as *Bebul*. Thus if the family celebrates any feast or function, the *bechas* everything on behalf of the house owner.

Tucha: This is another untranslatable title. Each Vaiphei family appoints two or more families in the village to be their *tuchas*. One family as head *tucha (tuchabul)* and others as junior *tuchas*. Whenever the family celebrates a feast or any function, the *tuchas* should serve the house. The *tuchas*, should be appointed from the families of the aunts (the father's or grand-father's sisters). Now if we see the chart, Kimbem's family can be appointed as *tucha* by the families of *Haupu, Haulian,* and Hauthang. So also Thanglet the son of Hoinu, Tongkam the son of Neikim can be appointed as *tucha* by these three families. However, Tongkam and Thanglet's families cannot appoint Kimbem and Veinu's families as their *tucha*. They can be appointed as *bechas*. Now the husband of Neikim and the husband of Hoinu are brothers because of their wives. This brotherhood is known as *nulam*. Now for example, I live at New Lambulane, Imphal and if I am to appoint some families to be my *tuchas*, I will have to appoint the families whose wives (mothers) are from Suantak clan. As I belong to Suantak clan, if a mother of a family is from Suantak clan I can appoint the family to be my *tucha*. My sisters will address my wife as *'hemou'* because the Vaipheis used this term *'hemou'* in addressing the wife of their brothers. If a woman addresses another woman as *'hemou'* (of course to a married woman), it means that she is addressing her as the wife of her brother. I can appoint the family of a woman who addresses my wife as *hemou*, to be my *tucha*.

Songgau is the family of our maternal uncle. e.g. I shall be *Songgau* in the house of my father's sister's family. So also to the families of my sisters. Traditionally, the *Songguas* were not supposed to go to the families of their aunties *(tuchas)* and if they go they were to eat outside the house of the *tuchas*. Now let us see the chart again. Haupu, Haulian and Hauthang are *Songgaus* in the house (families) of Kimbem (if married), Tongka.,

Thanglet and Veinu (after marriage). They are in turn *tuchas* in the houses of the formers. It is below his dignity if one *Songgau* expects something from the *tucha* or requests him to give something. However, it is the privilege of a *tucha* to expect gifts from the *Songgaus*. E.g. My sisters and their children have every right to come and ask me to buy something for them. However it will be below our dignity if my children (my family) request the *tuchas* to buy something for us.